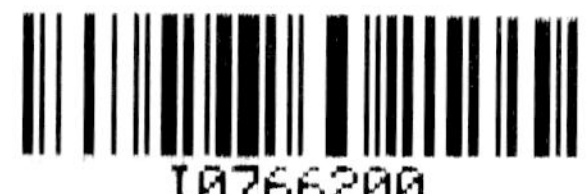

Edited by Sabrine Micha Na
Layout by Vagner Lopes
Photographs by Ymfargon

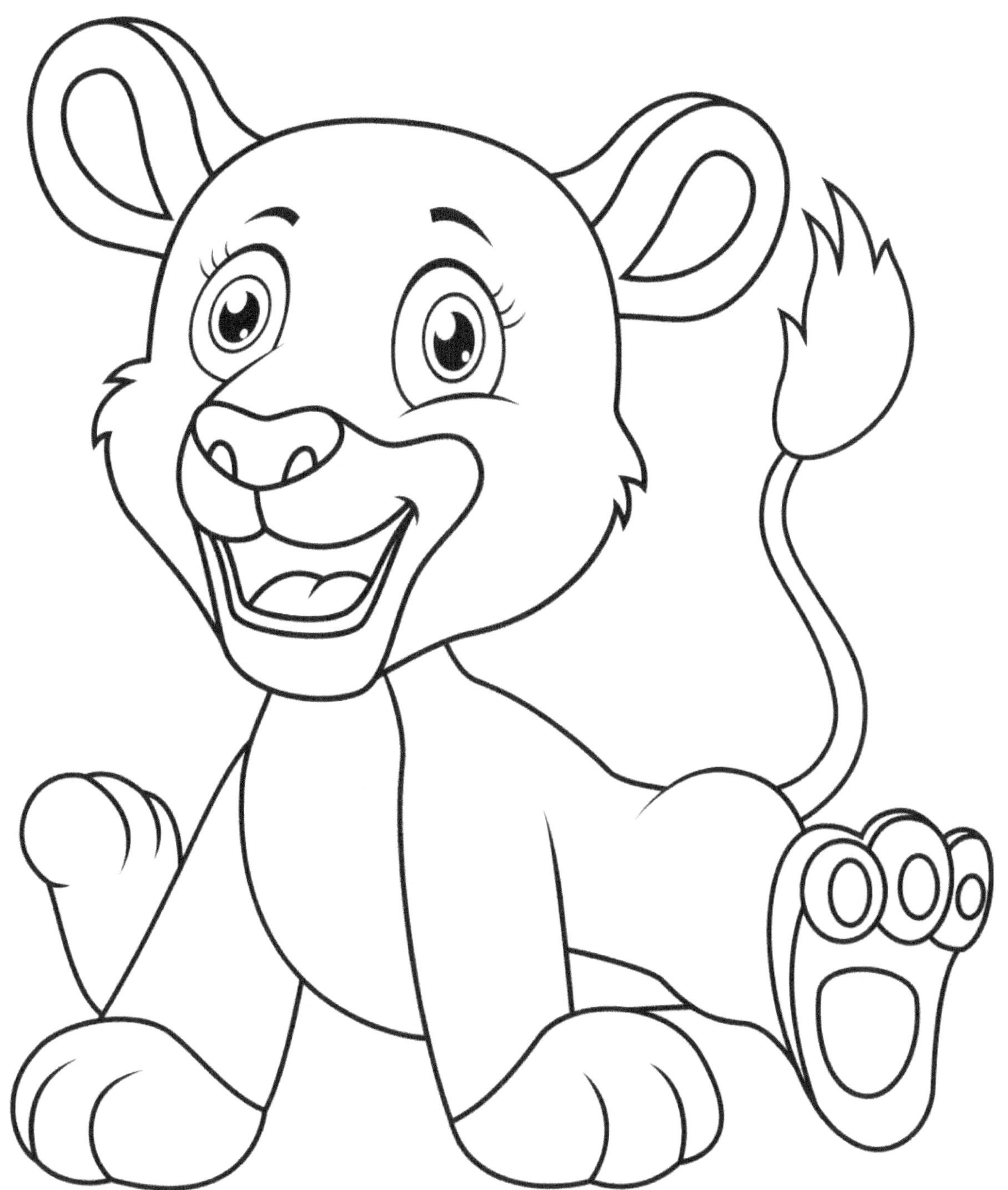

This book belongs to :

. . . .

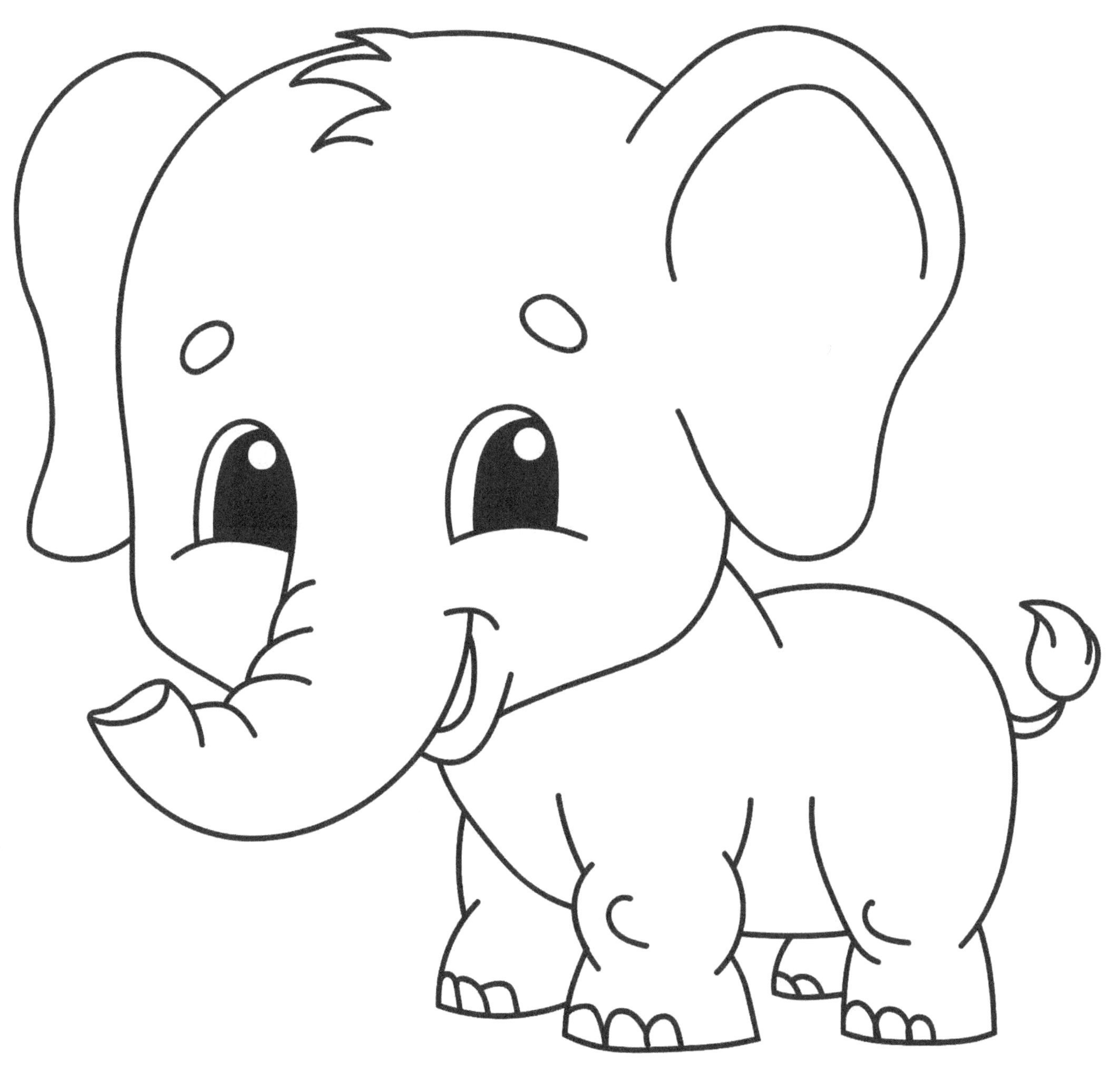

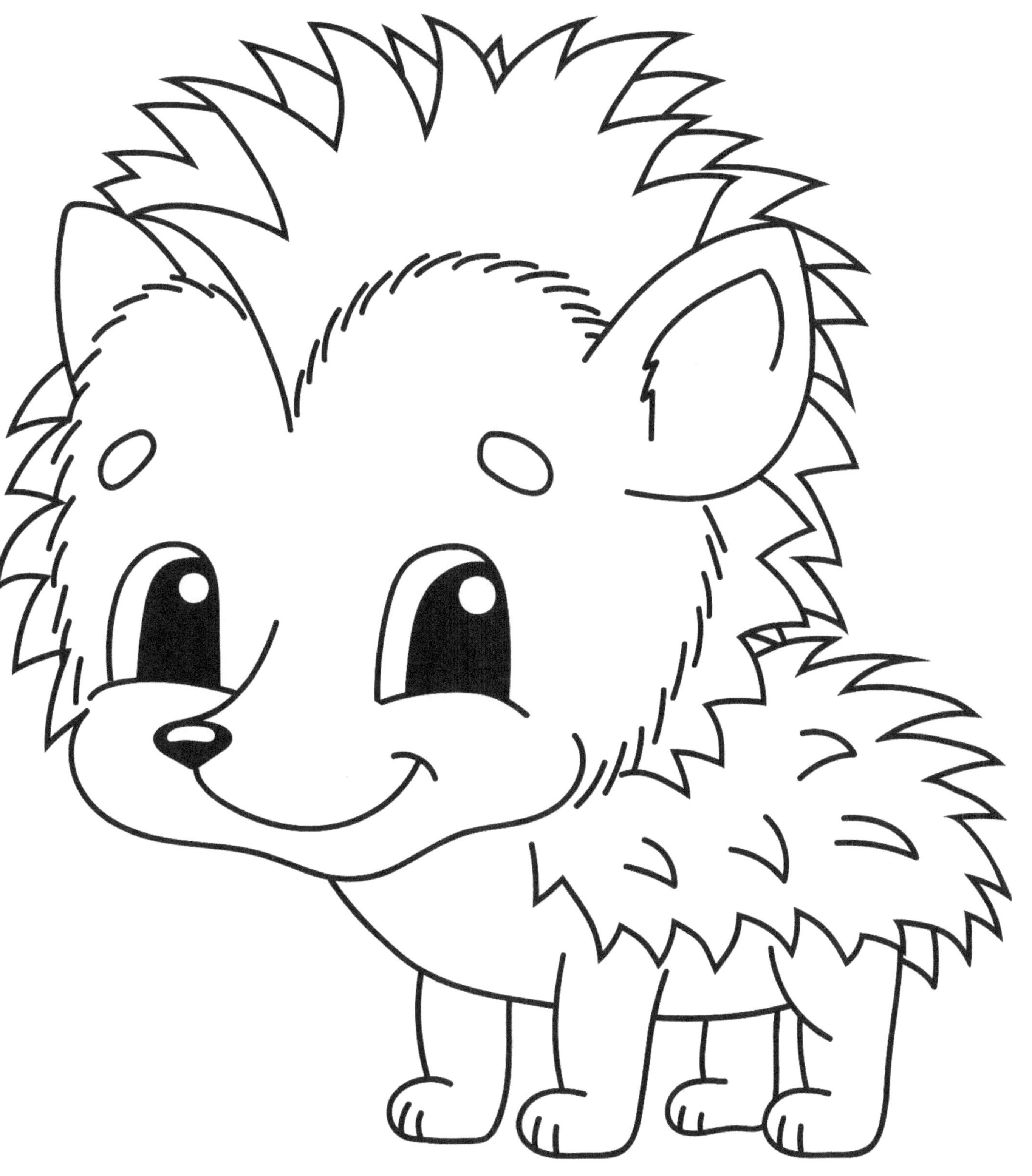

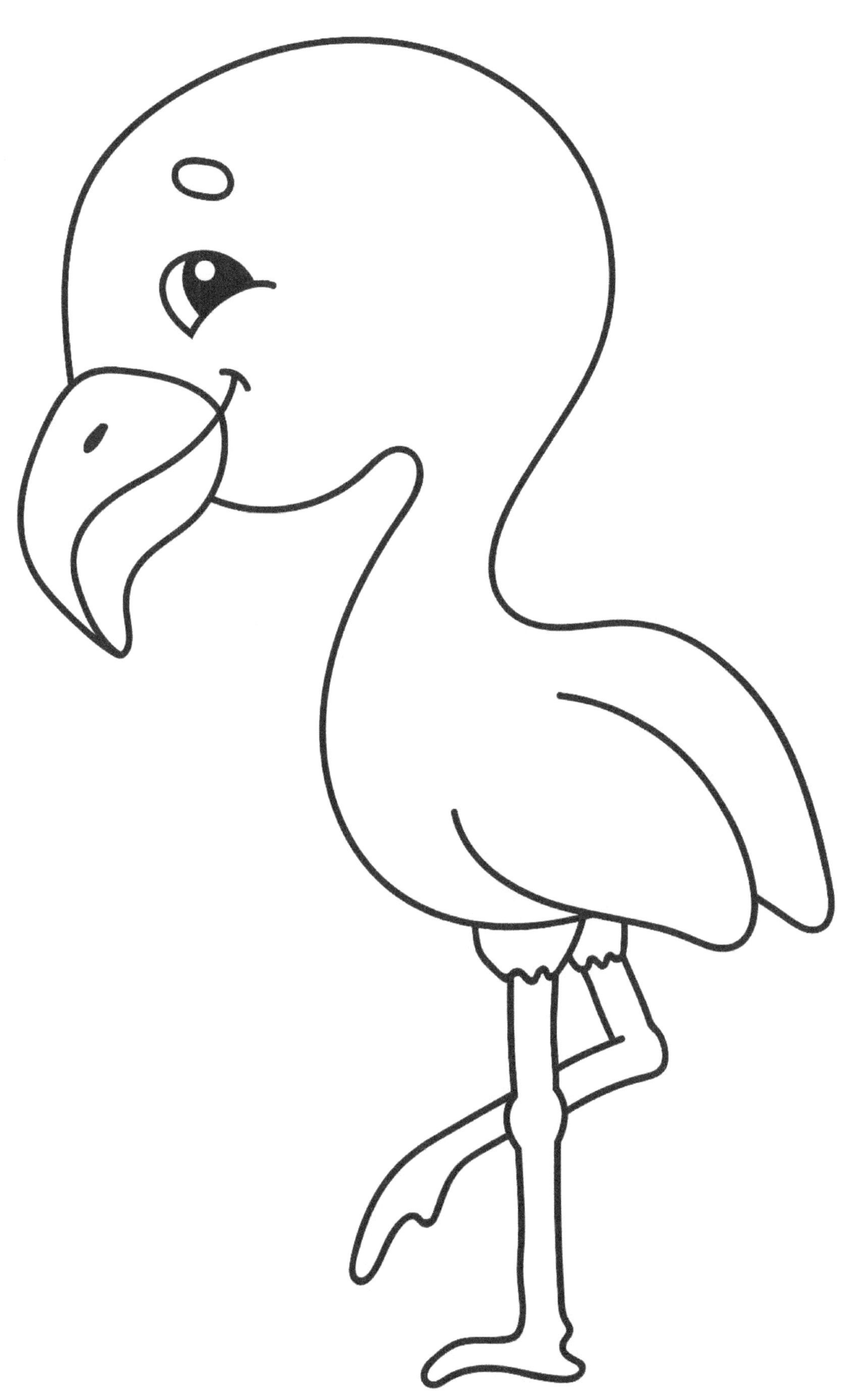

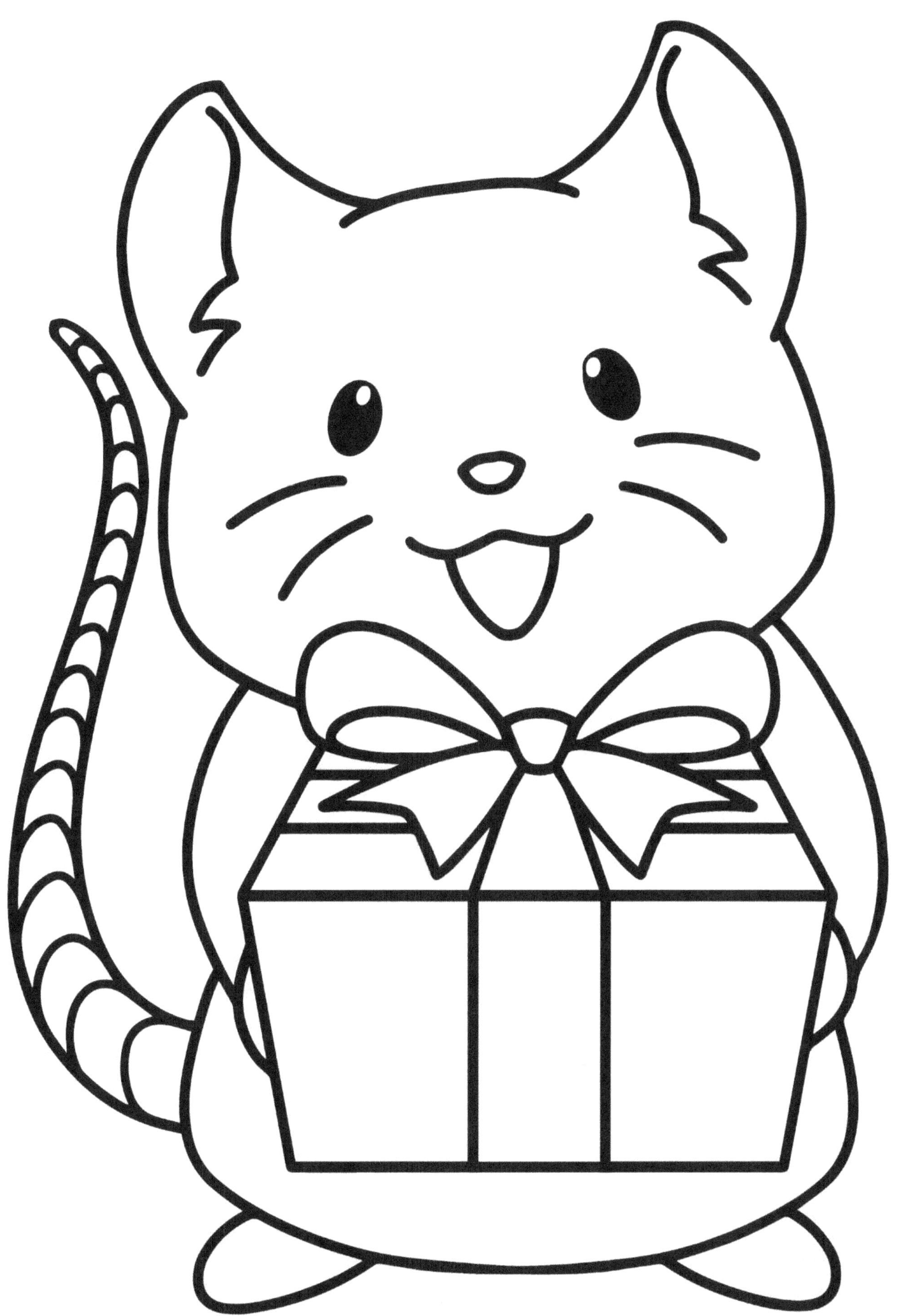

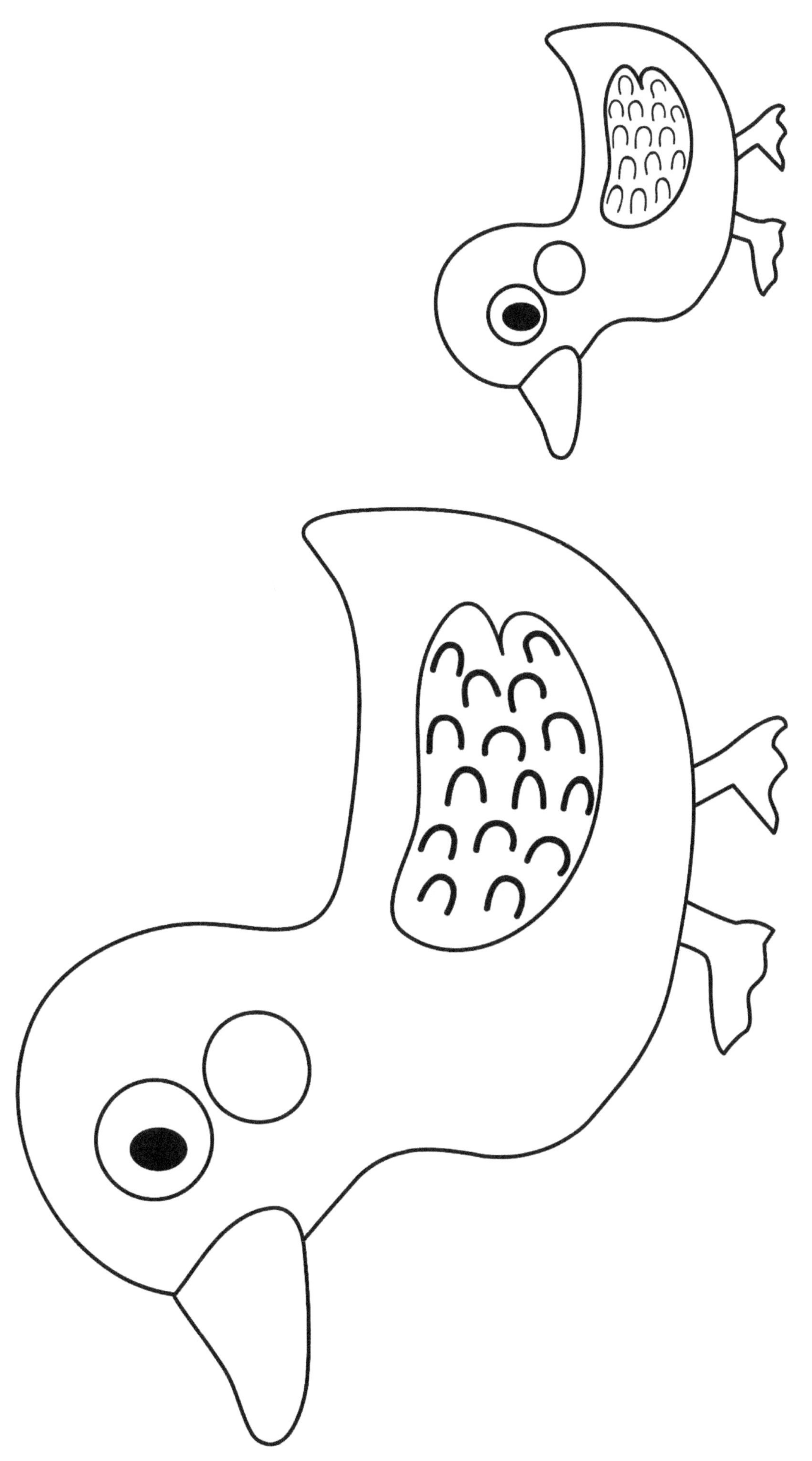

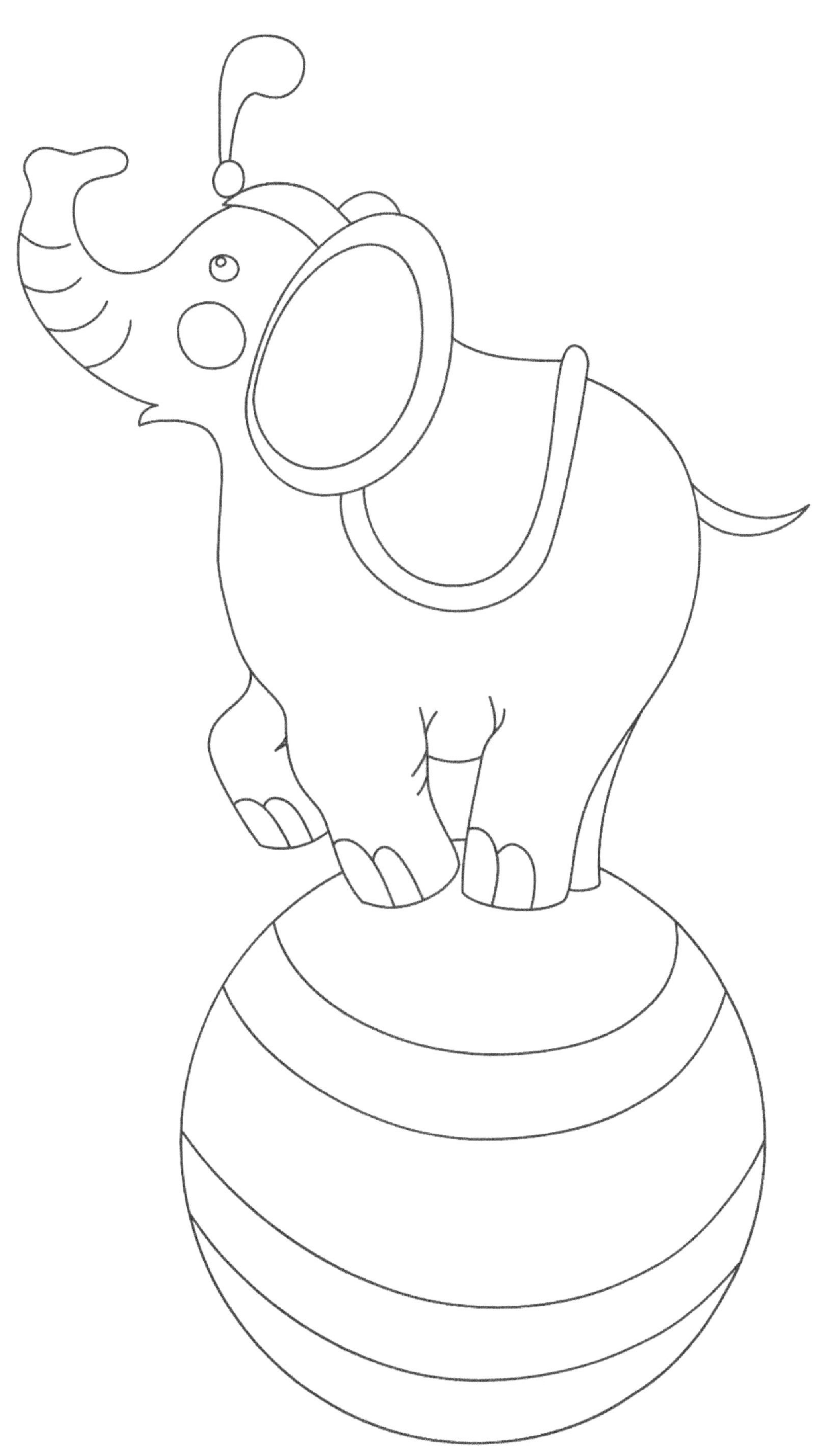

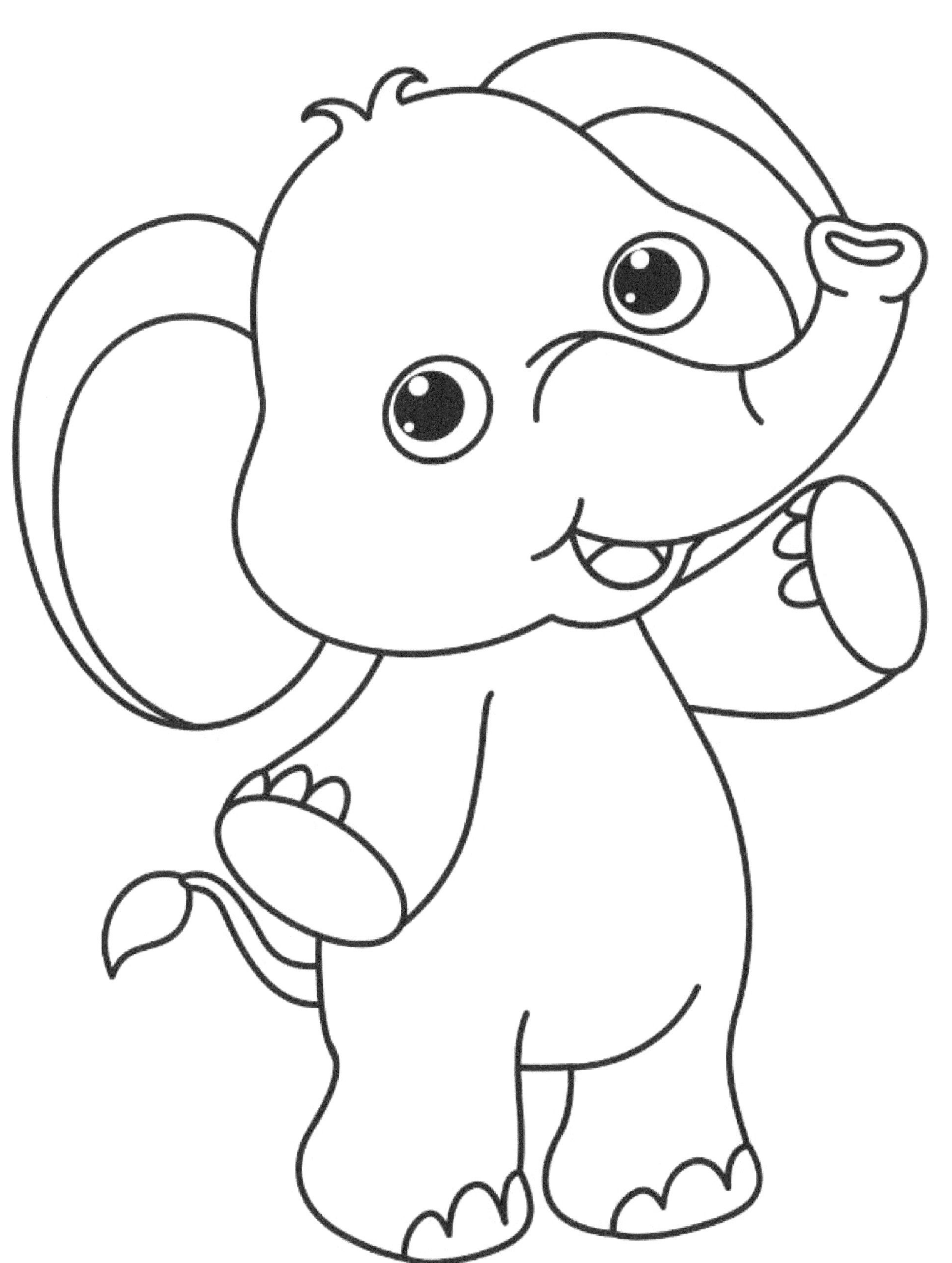

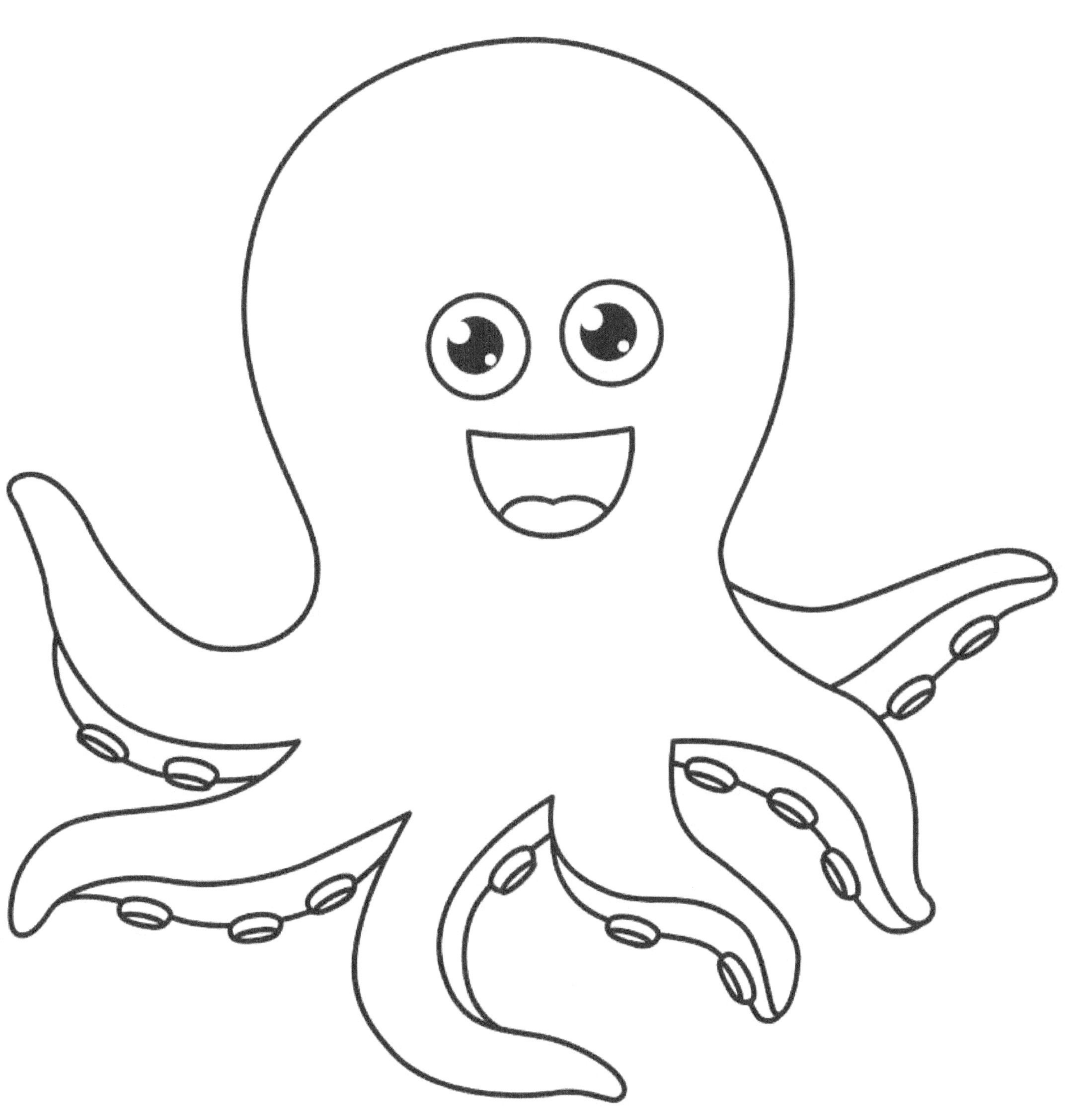

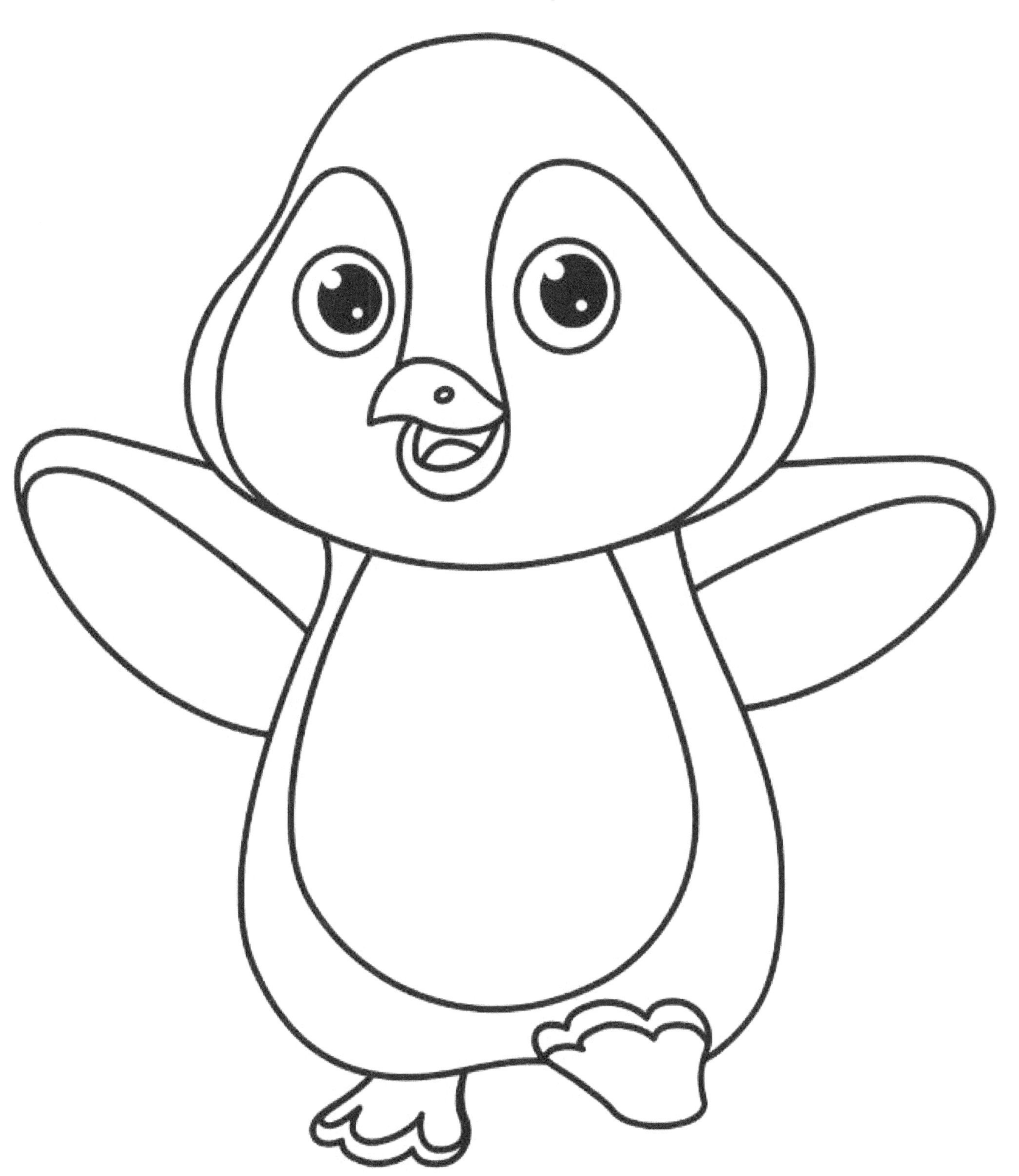

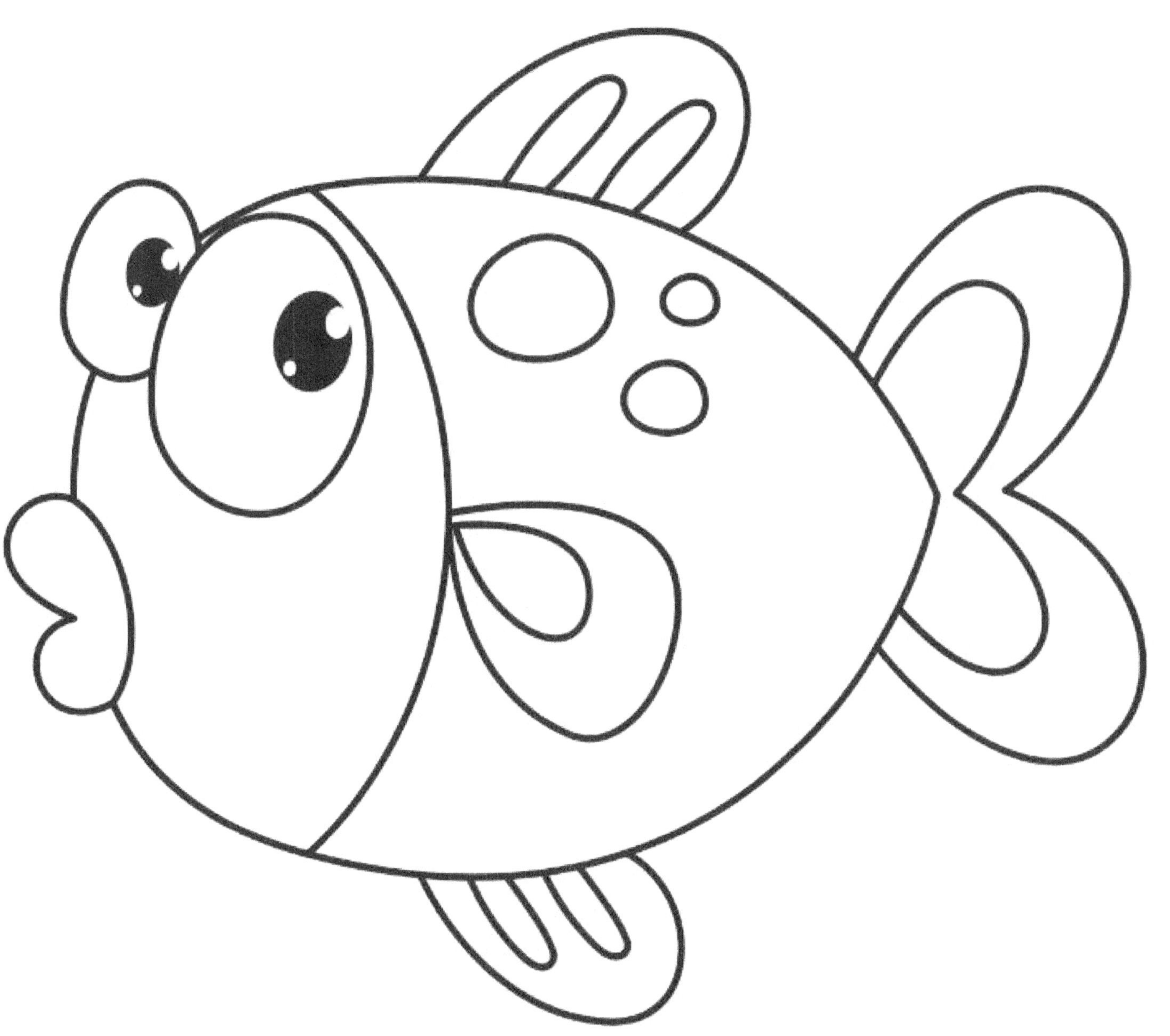

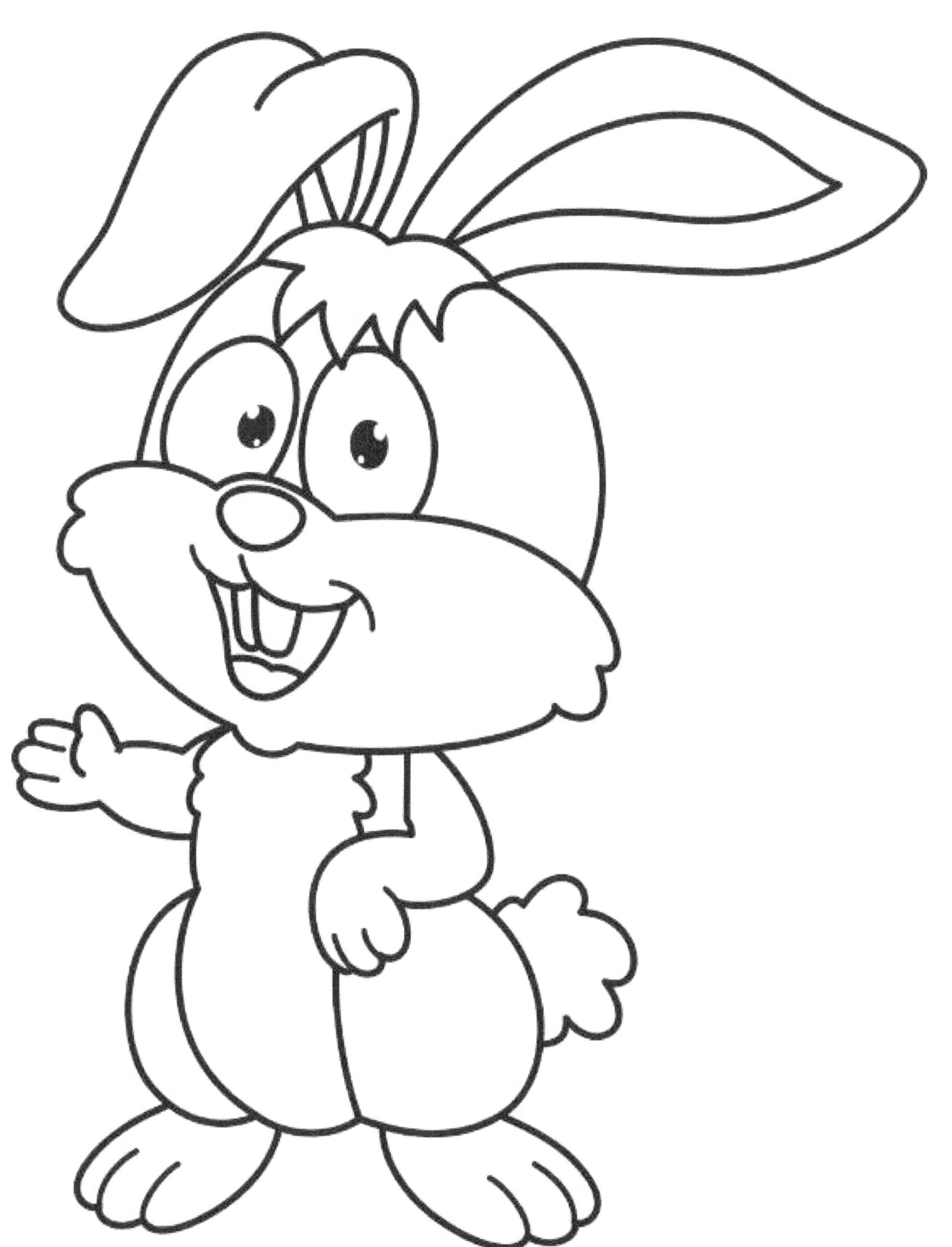

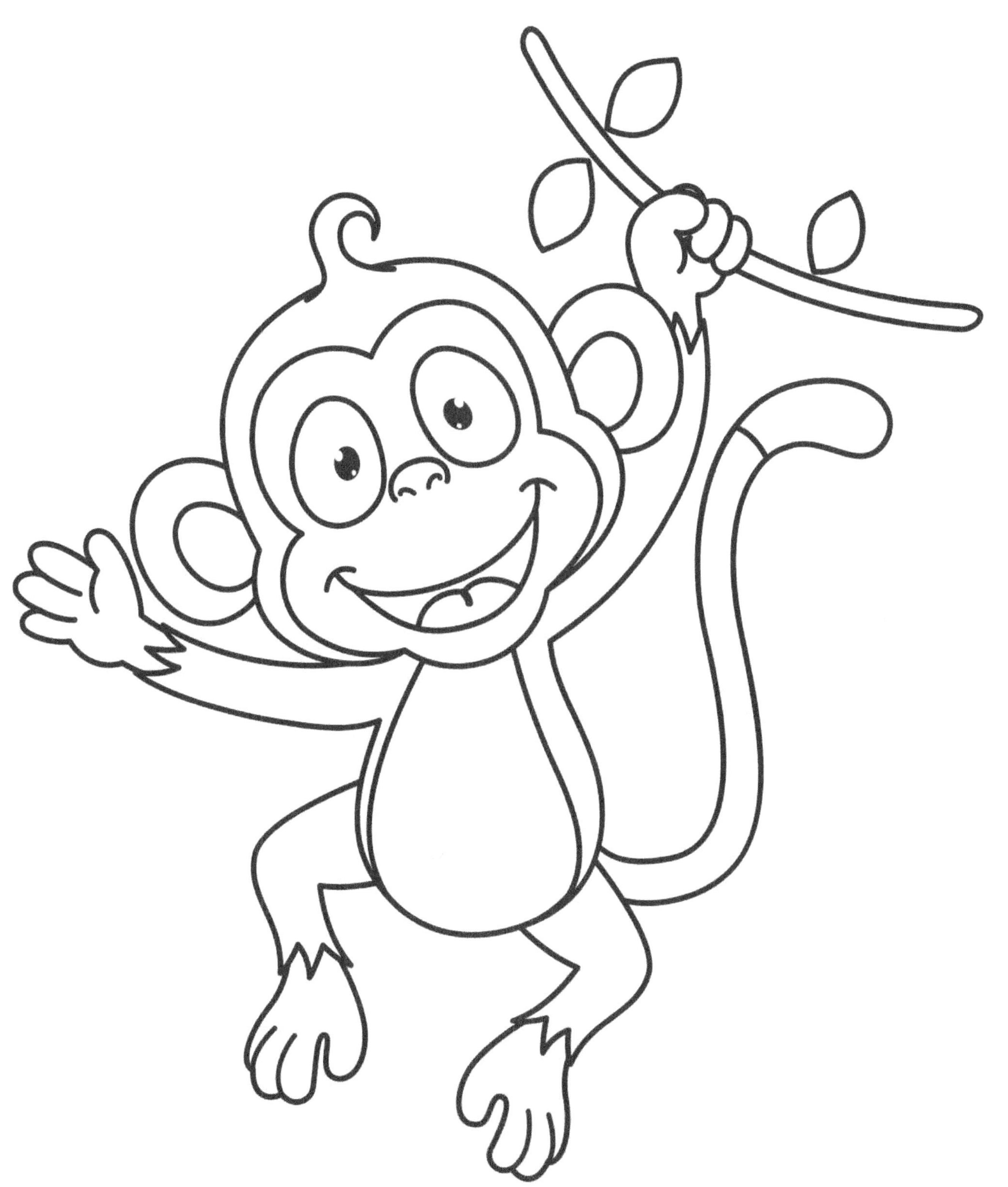

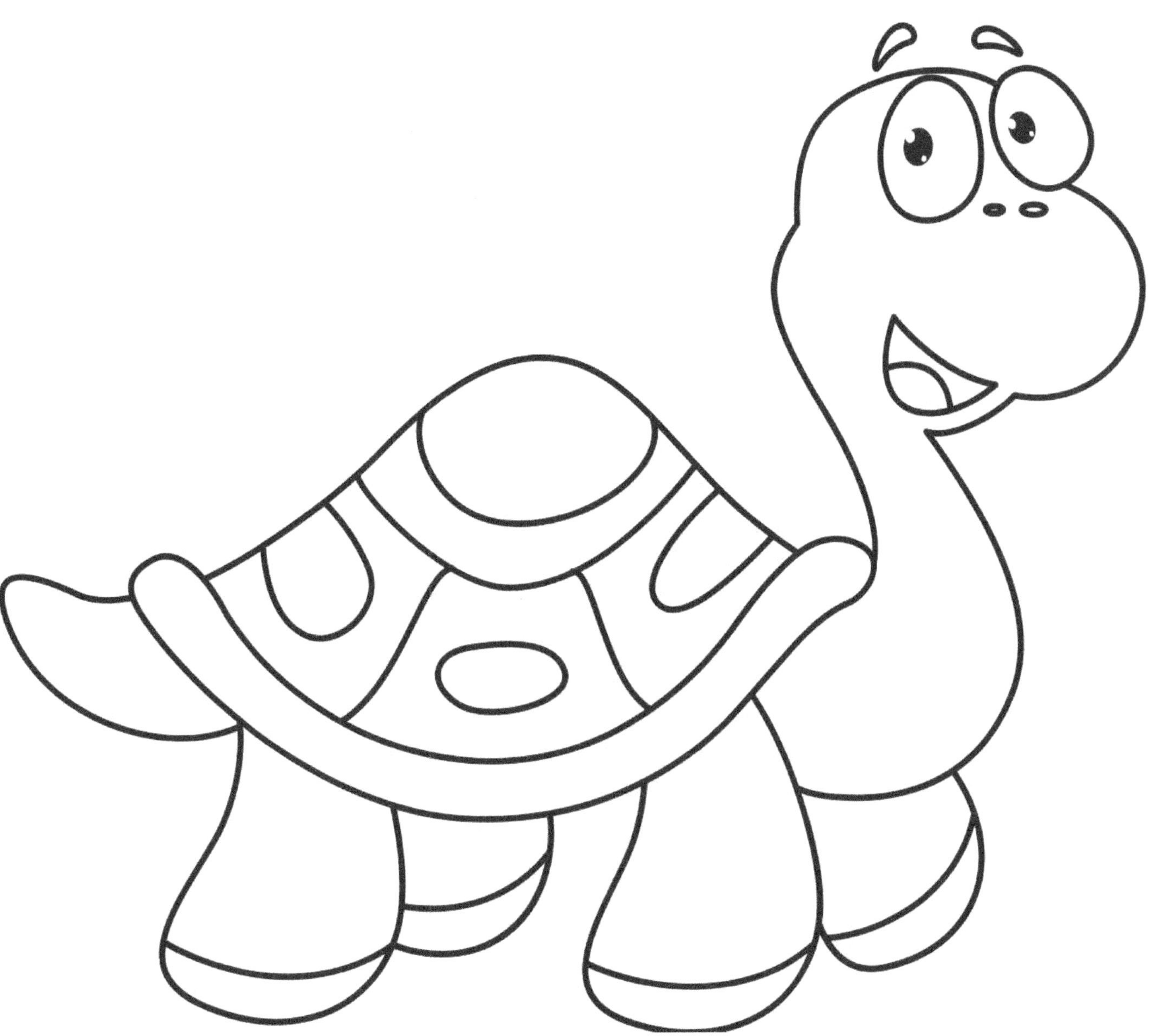

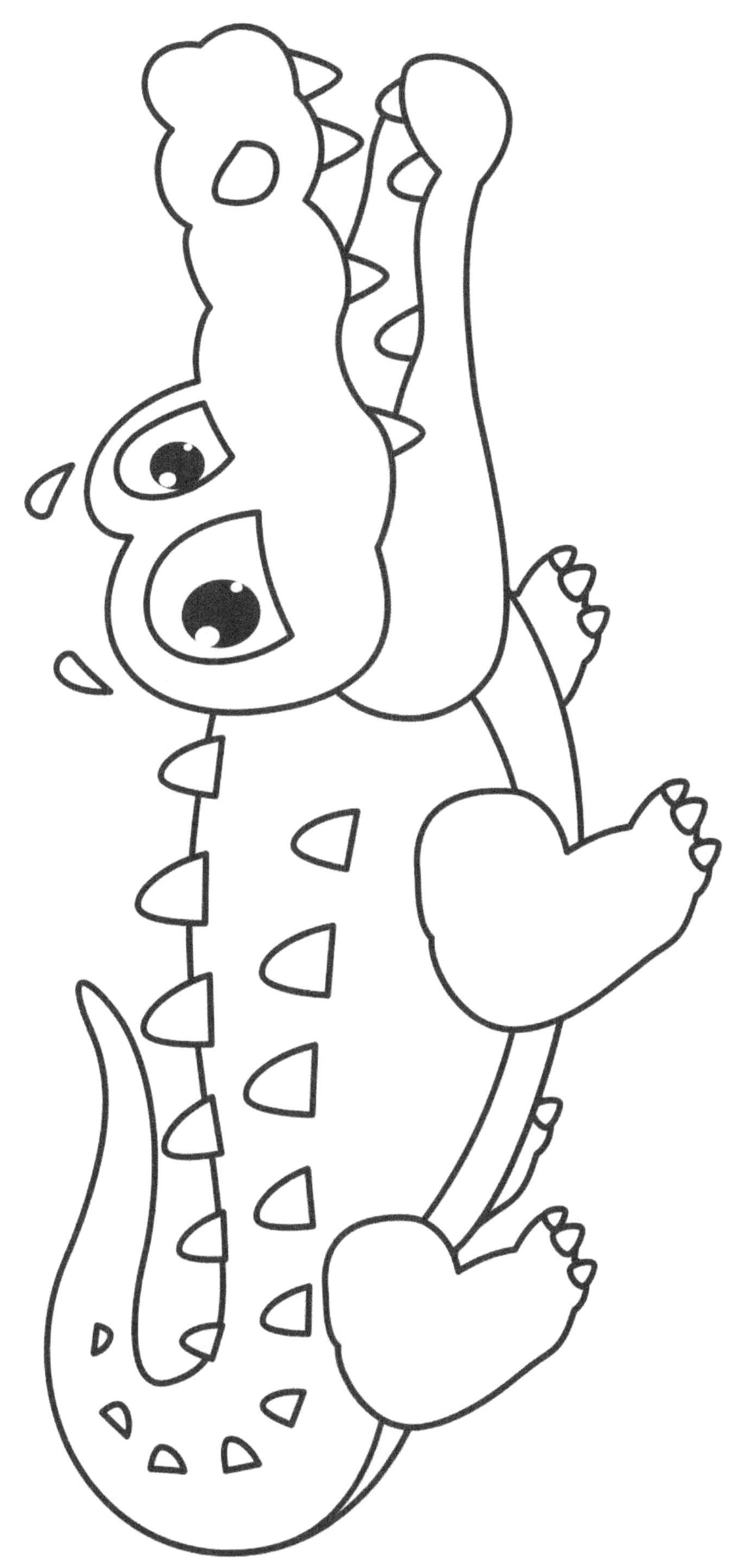

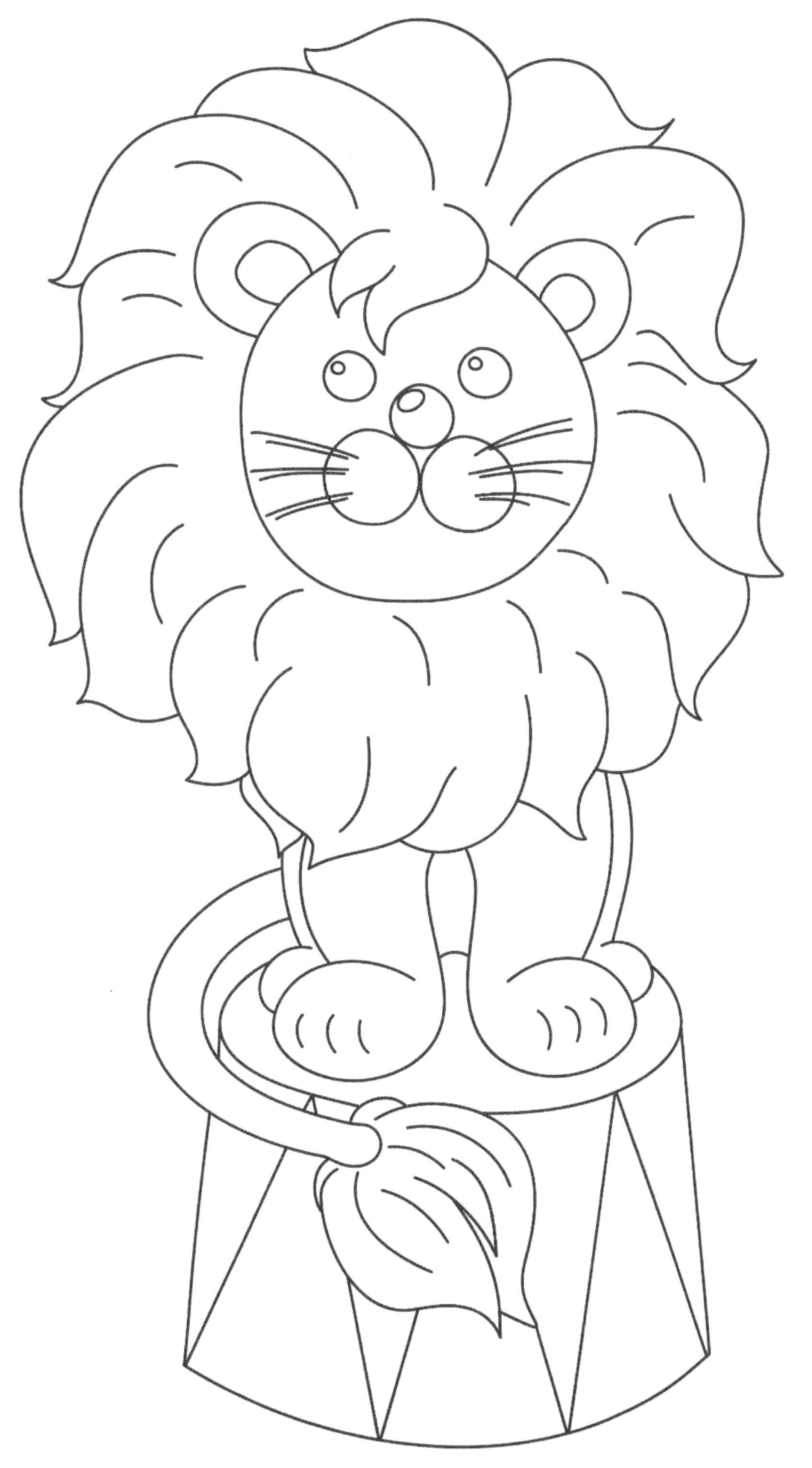

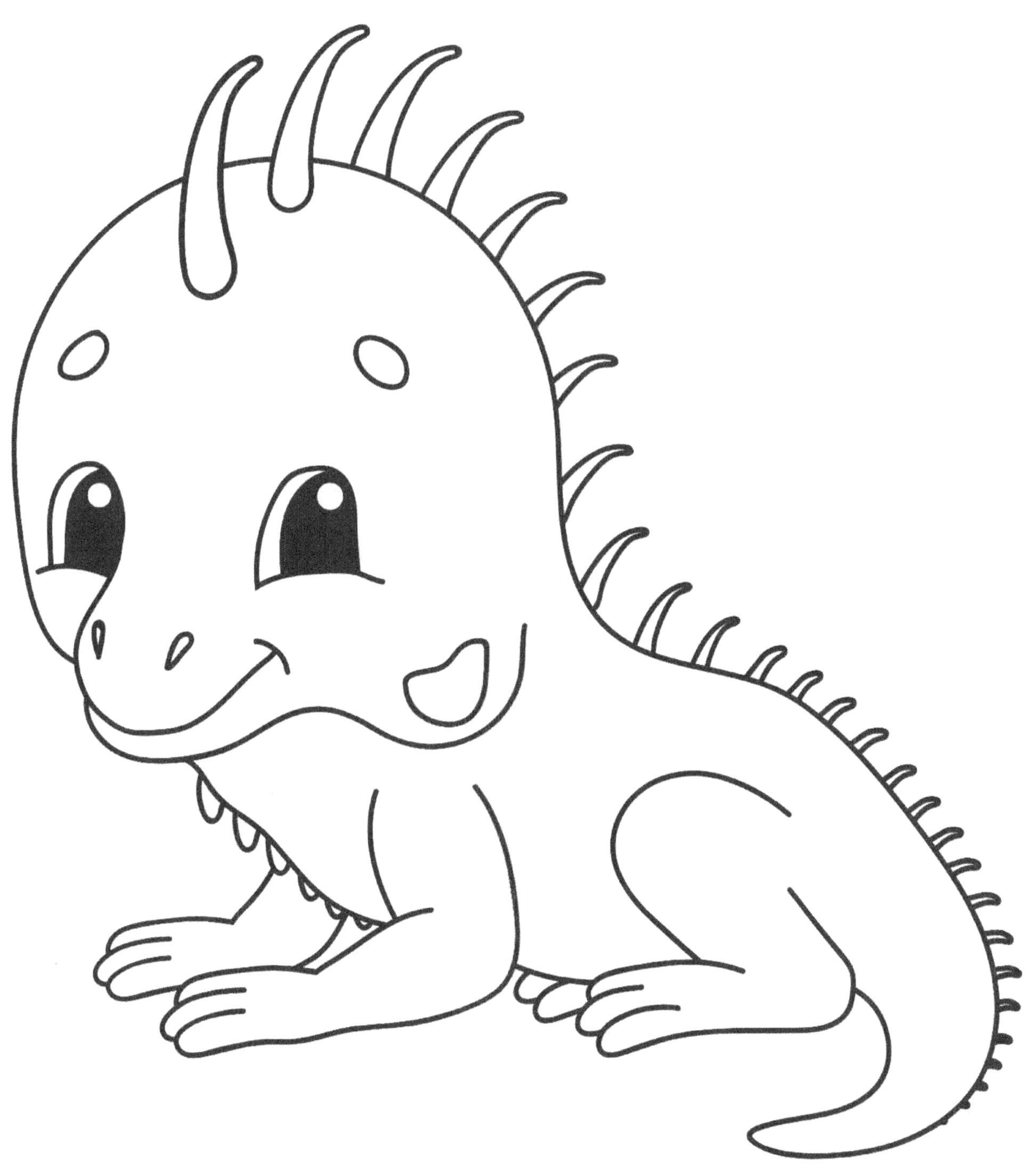

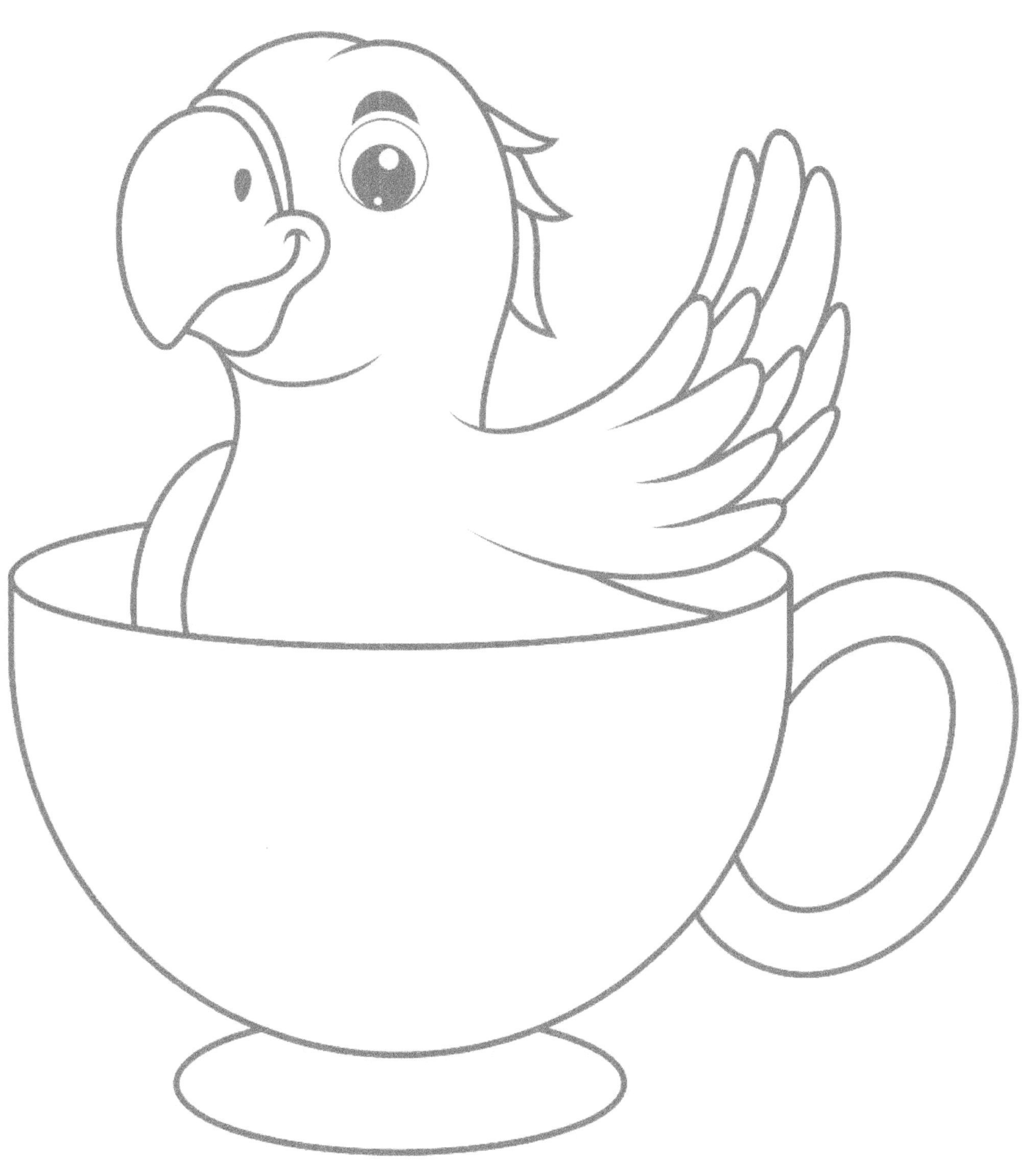

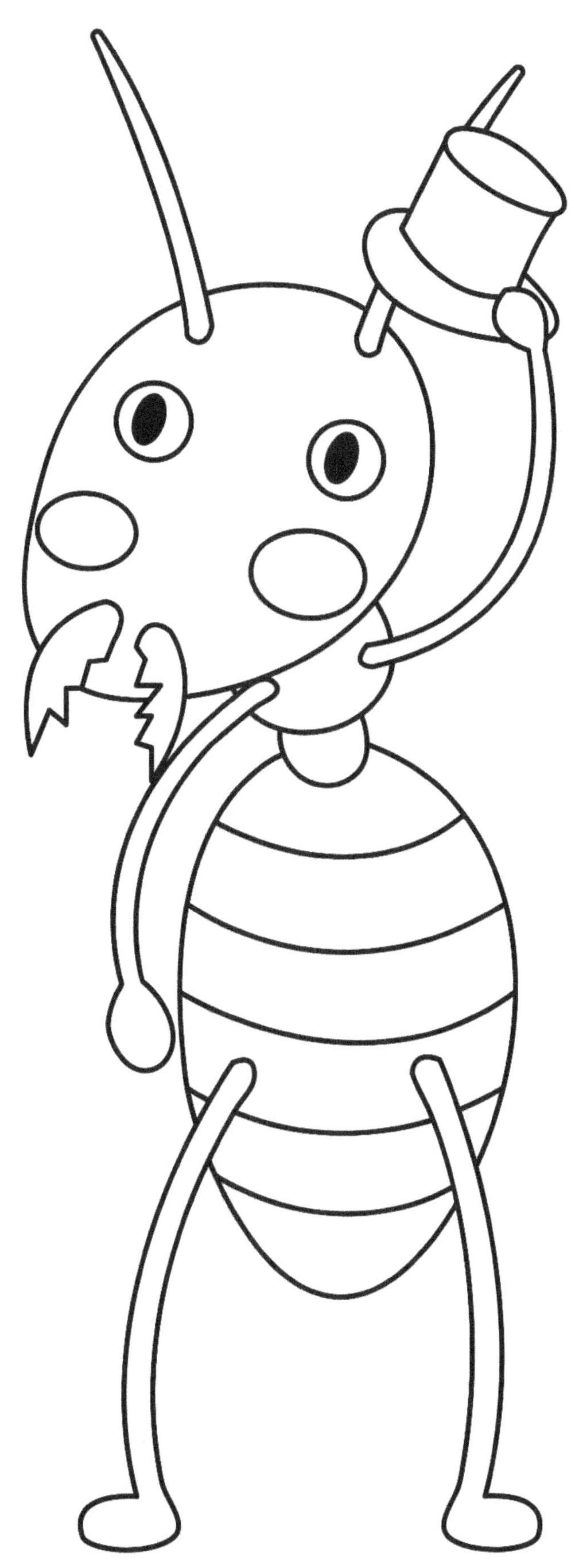

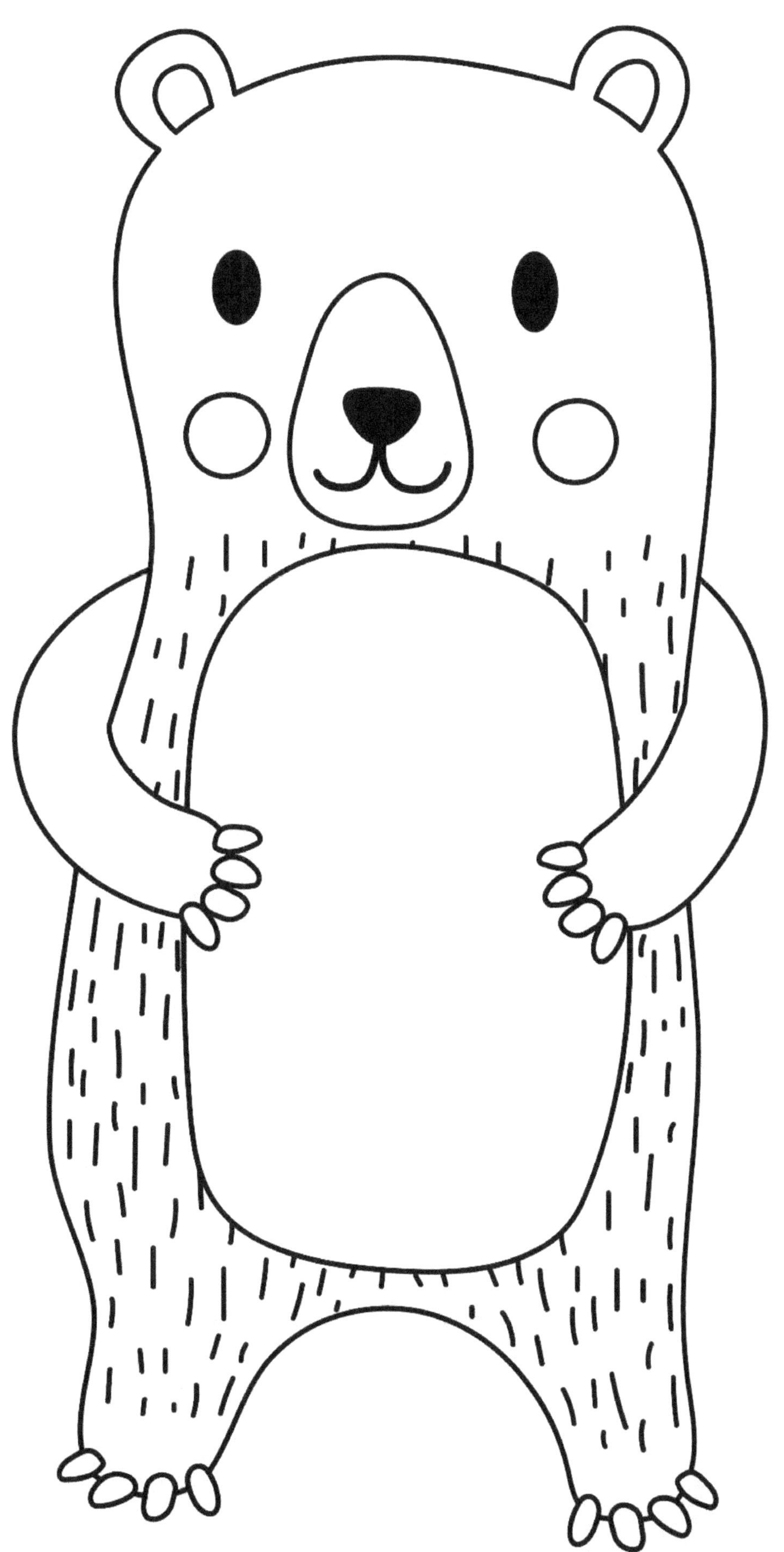

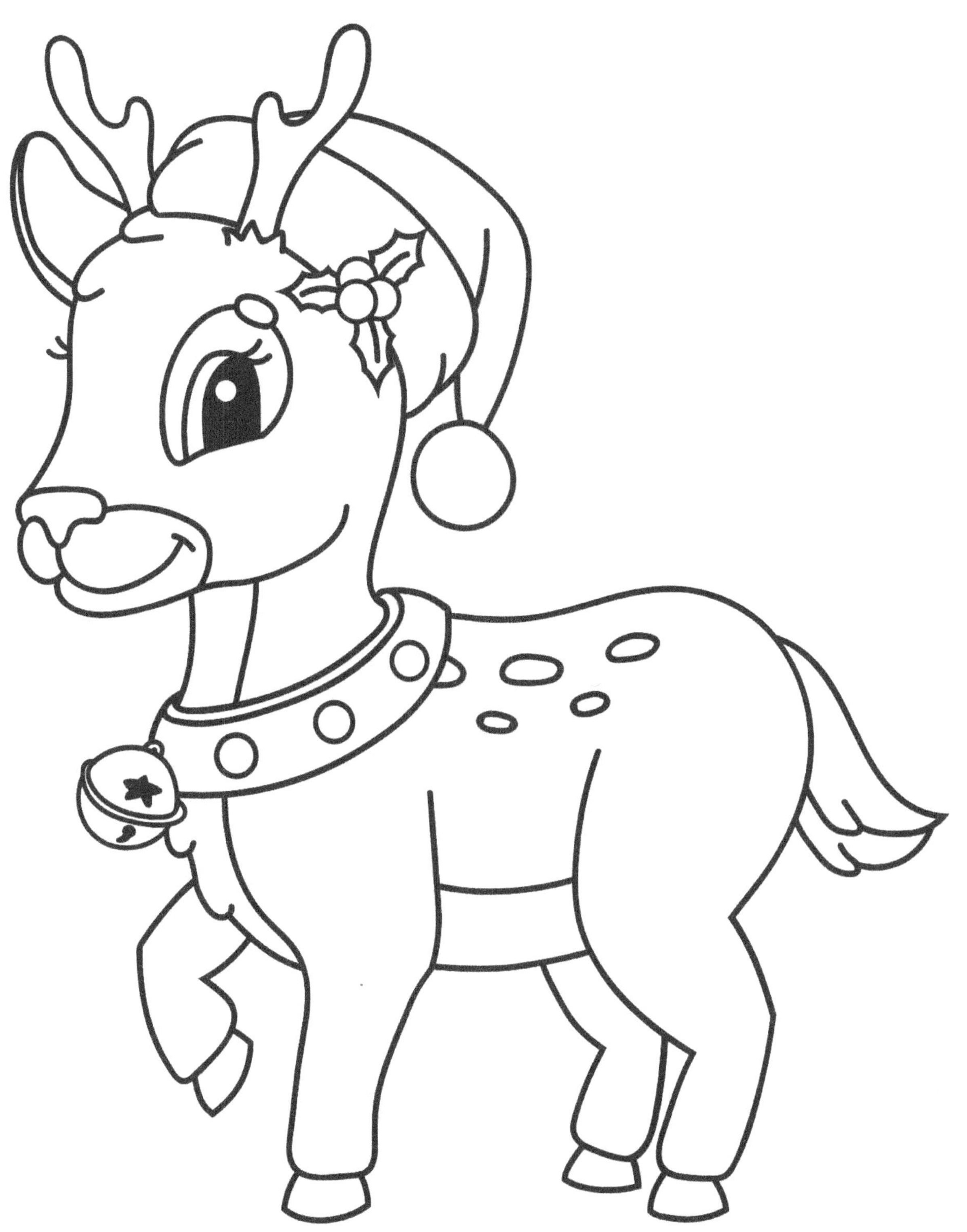

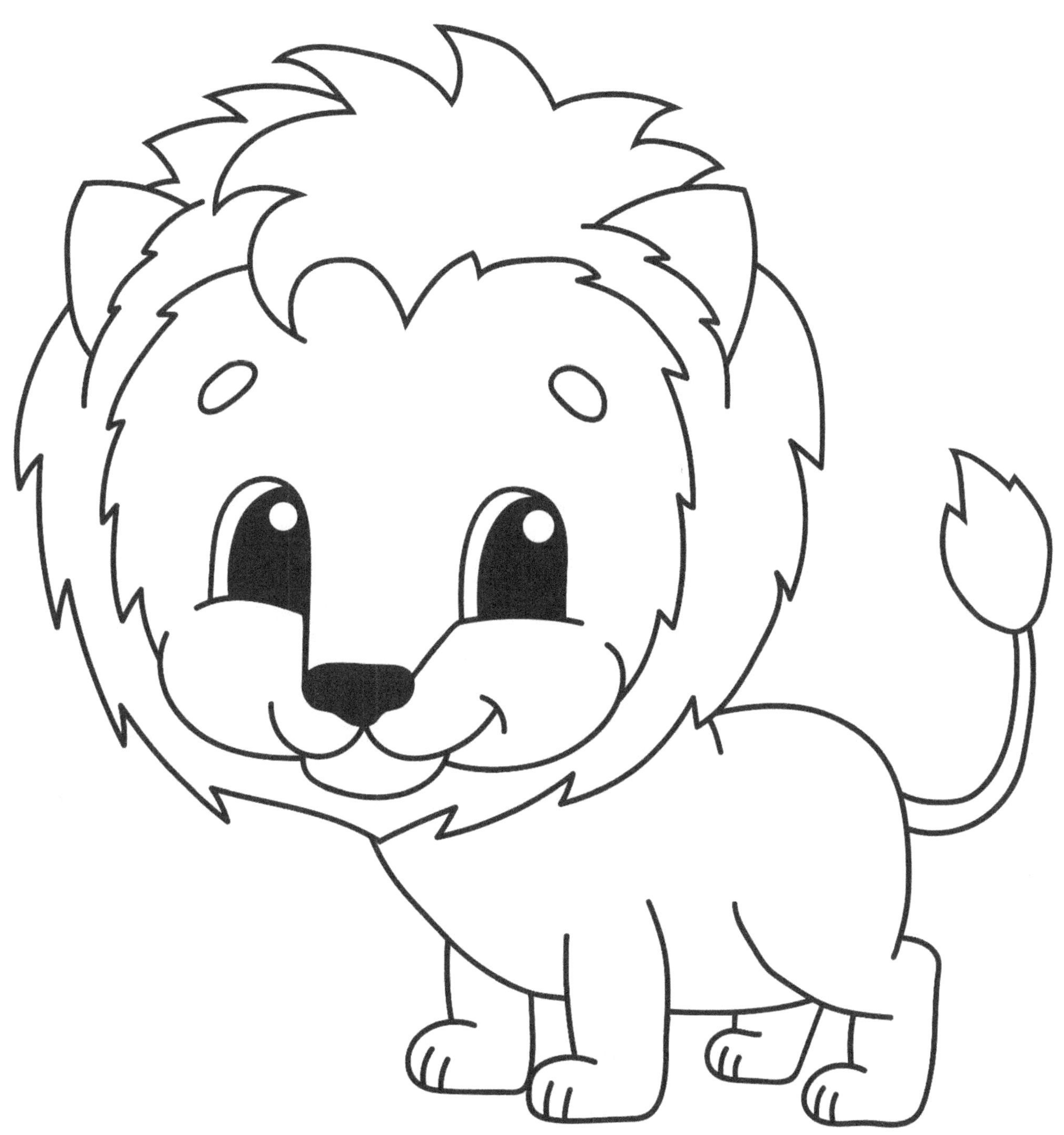

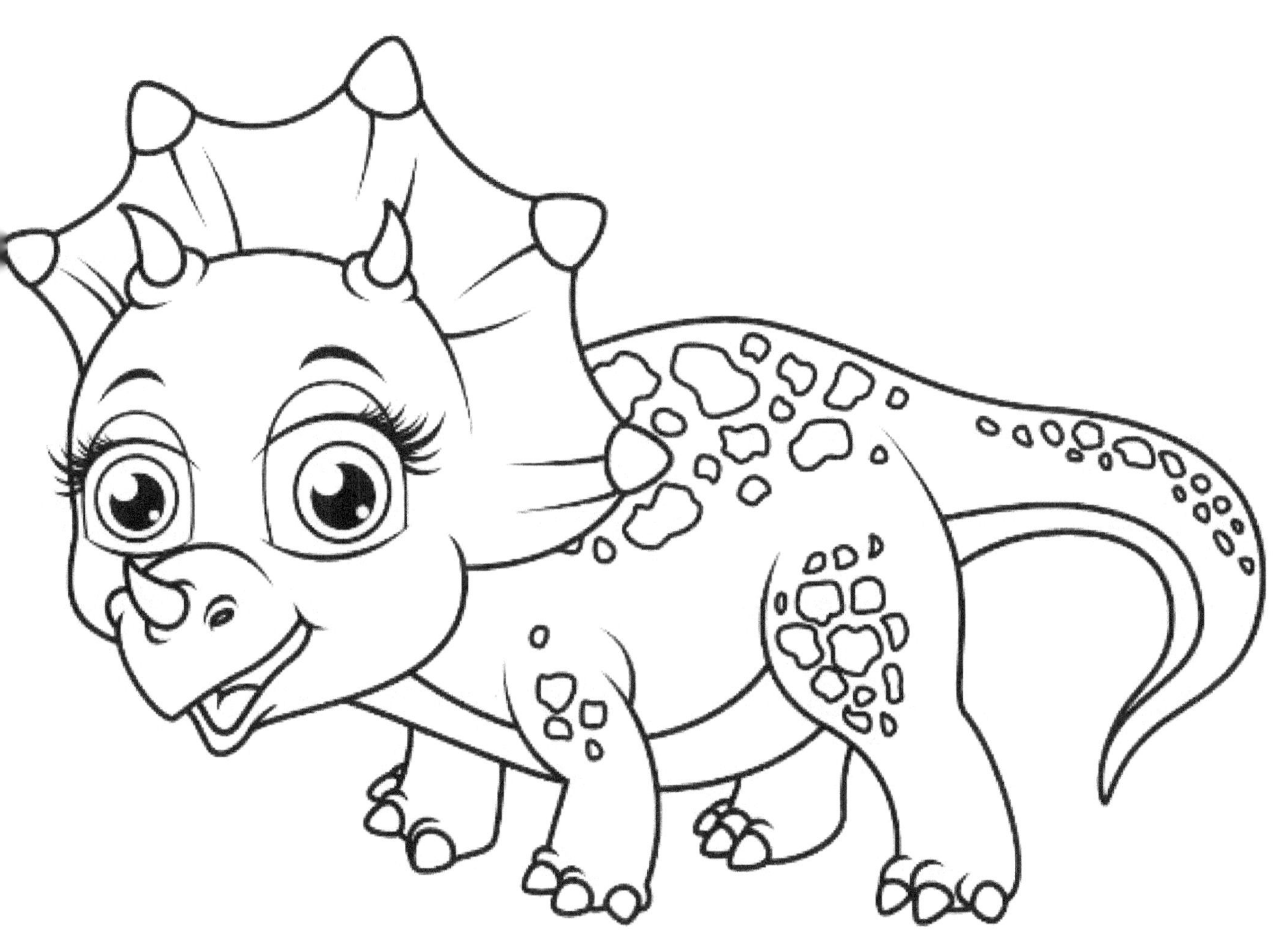

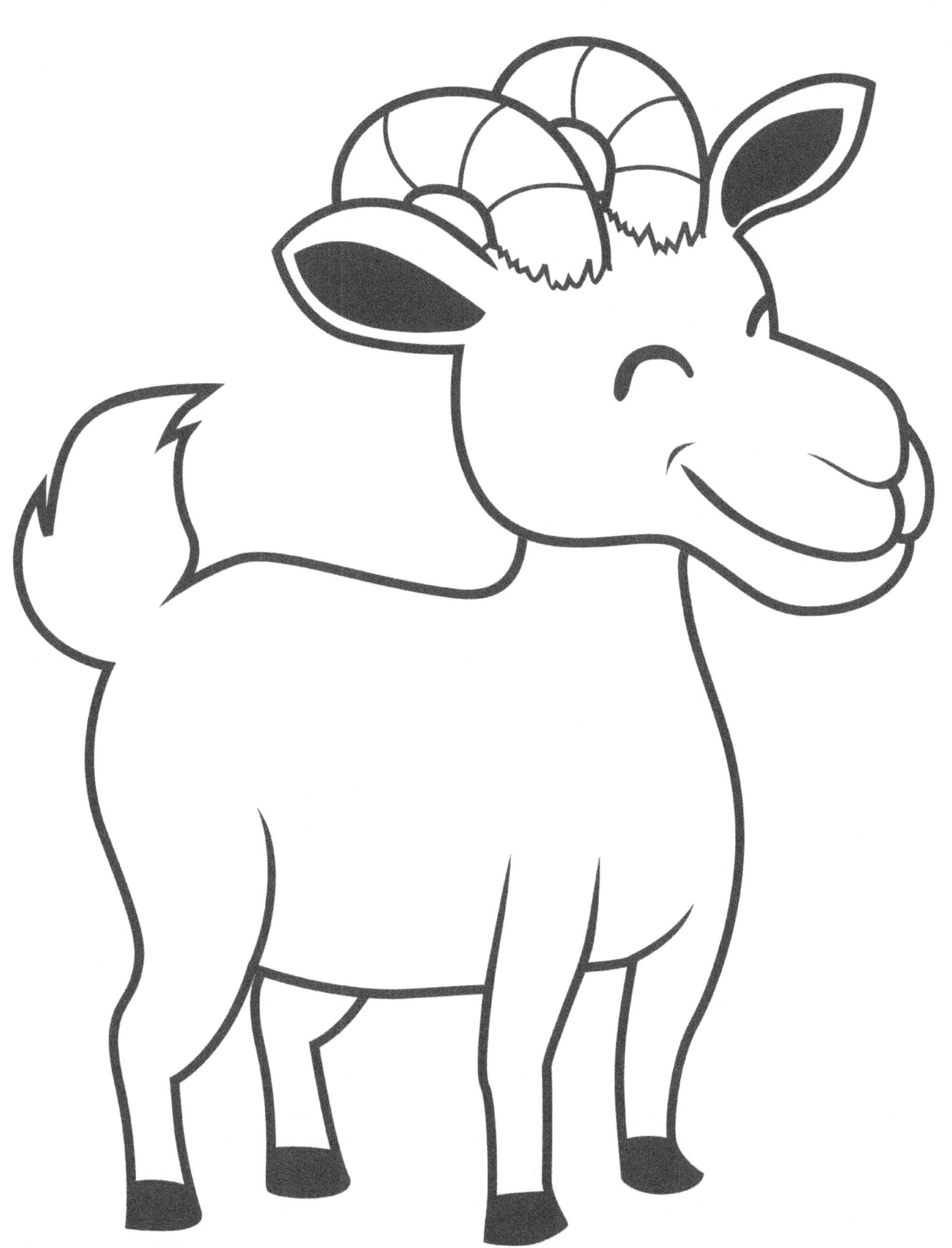

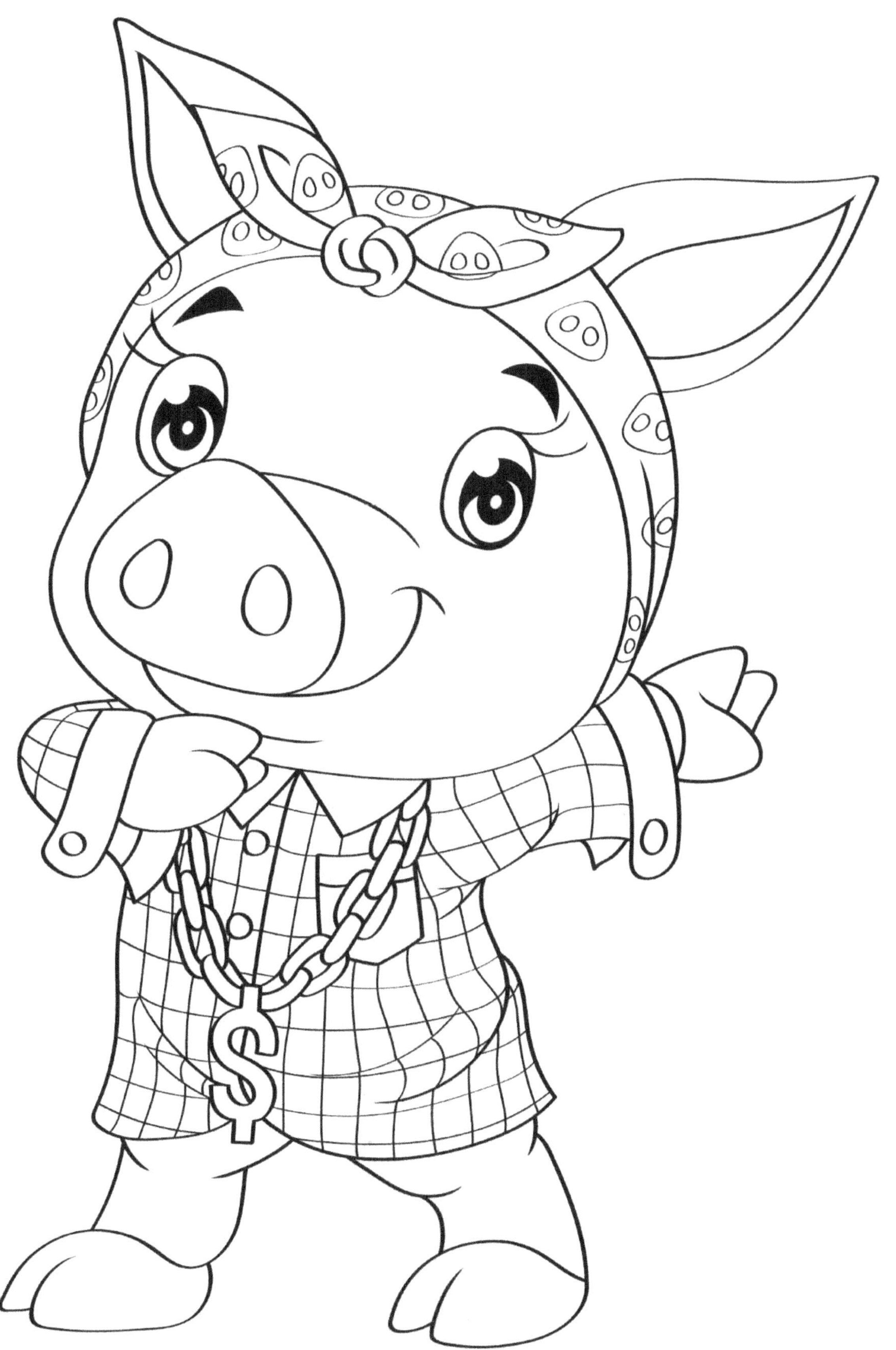

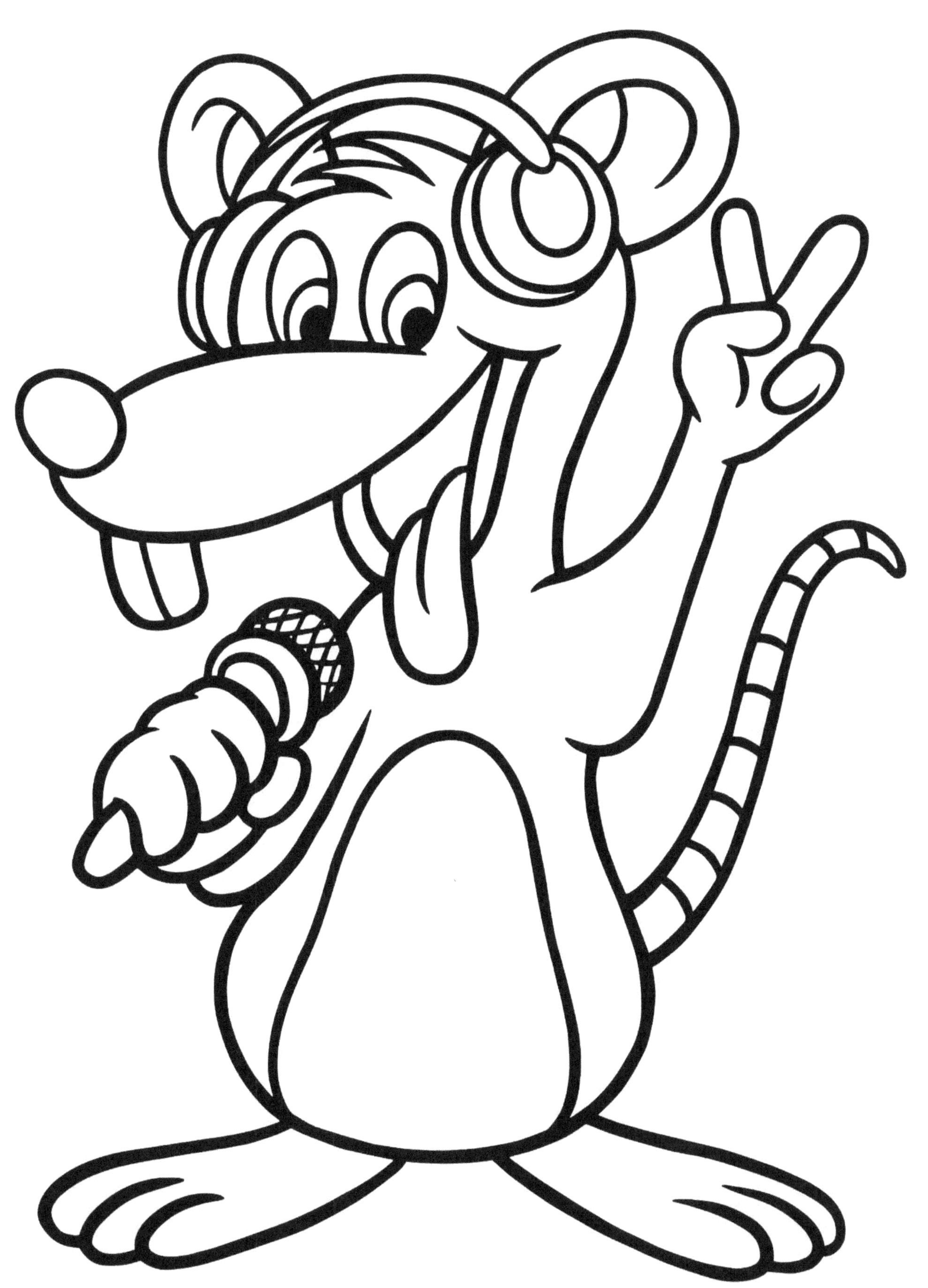

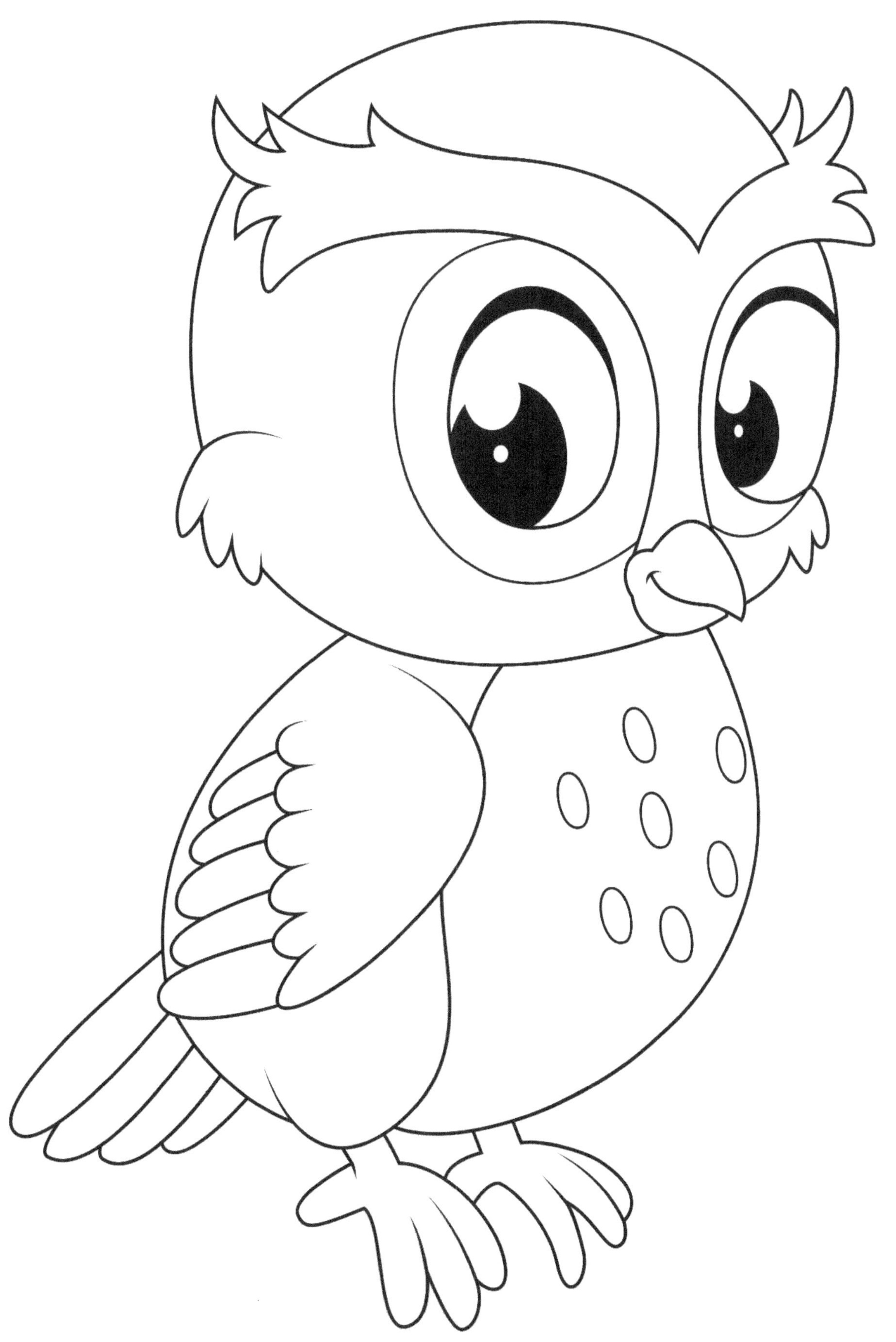

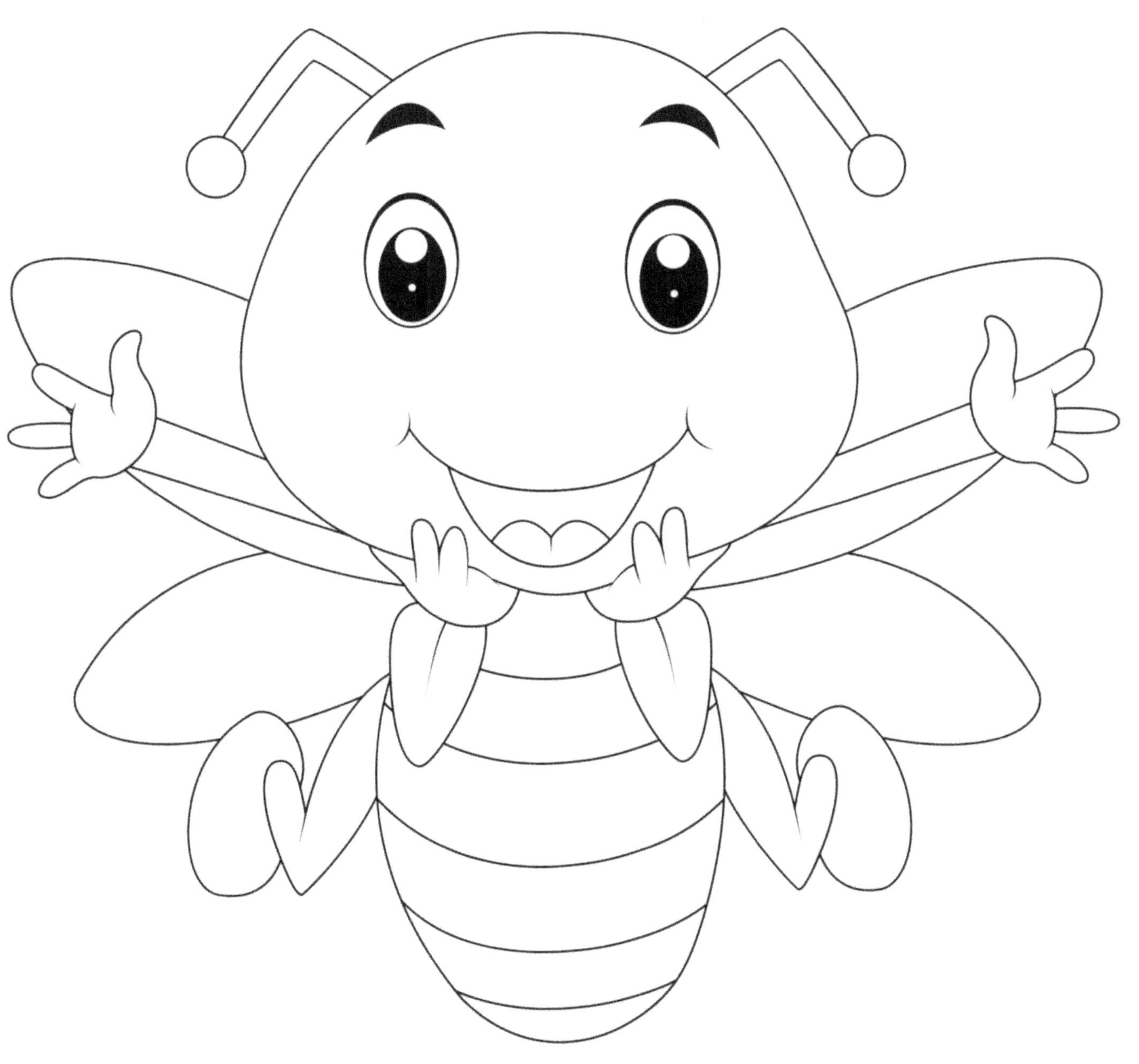

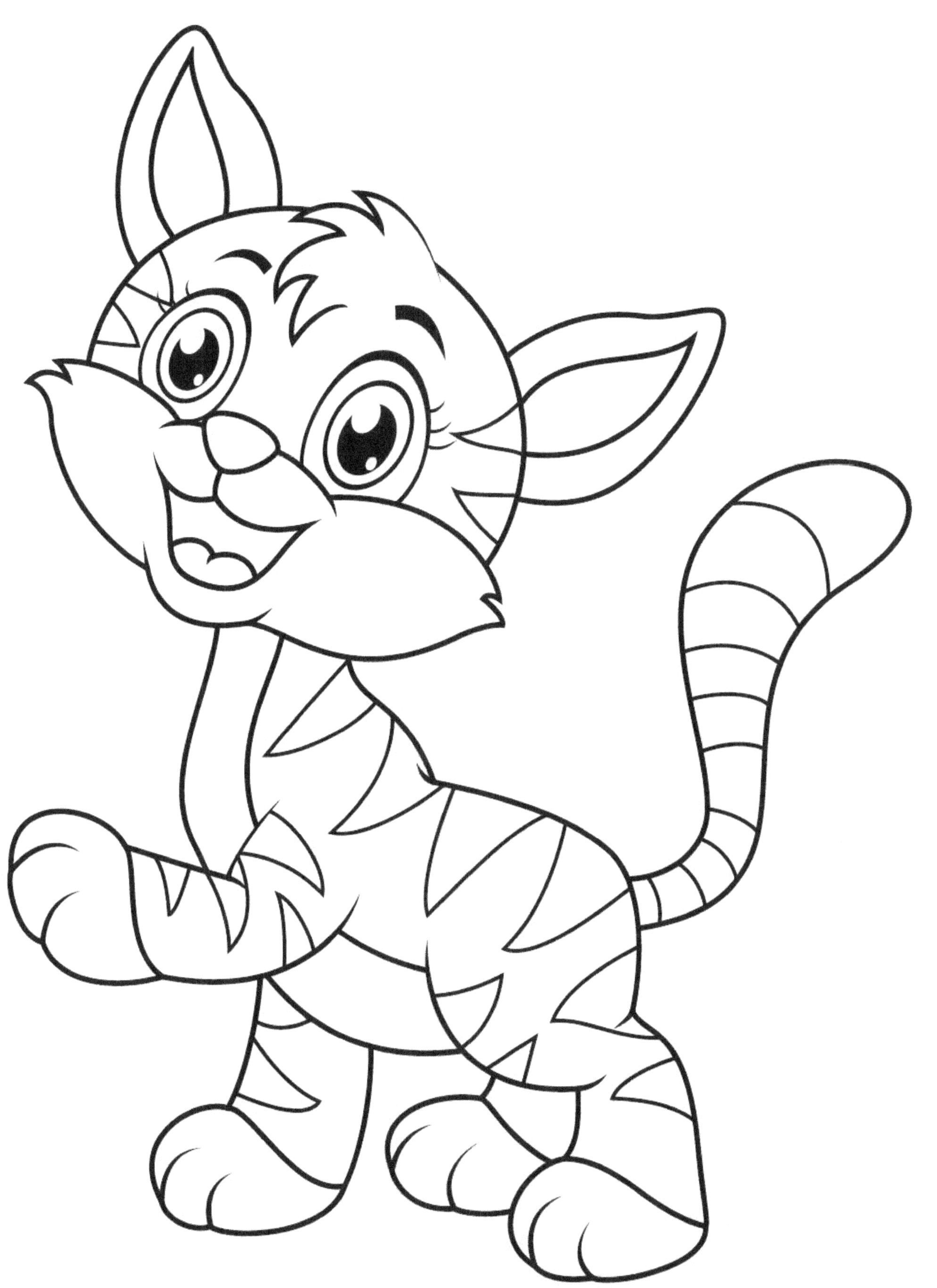

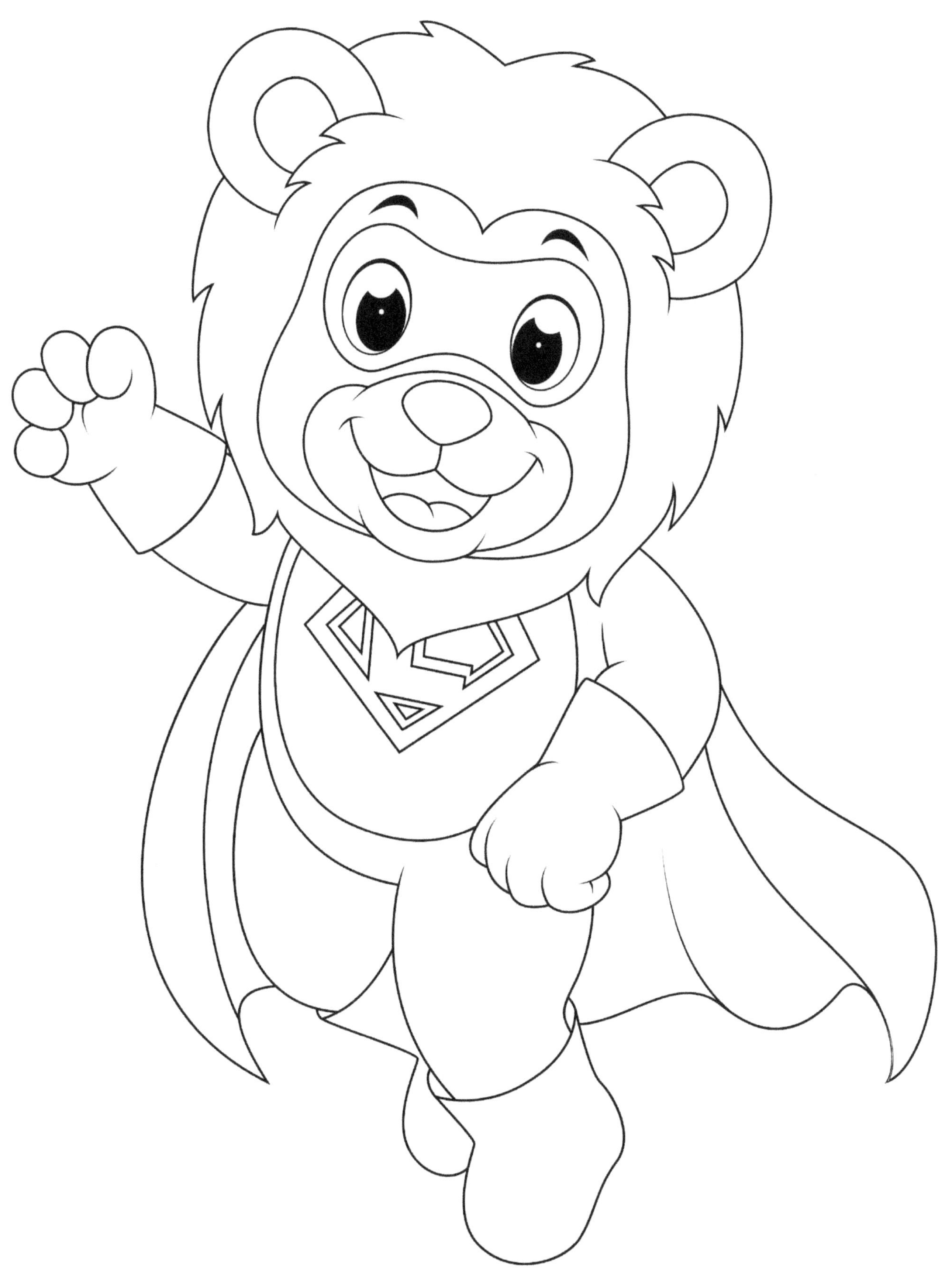

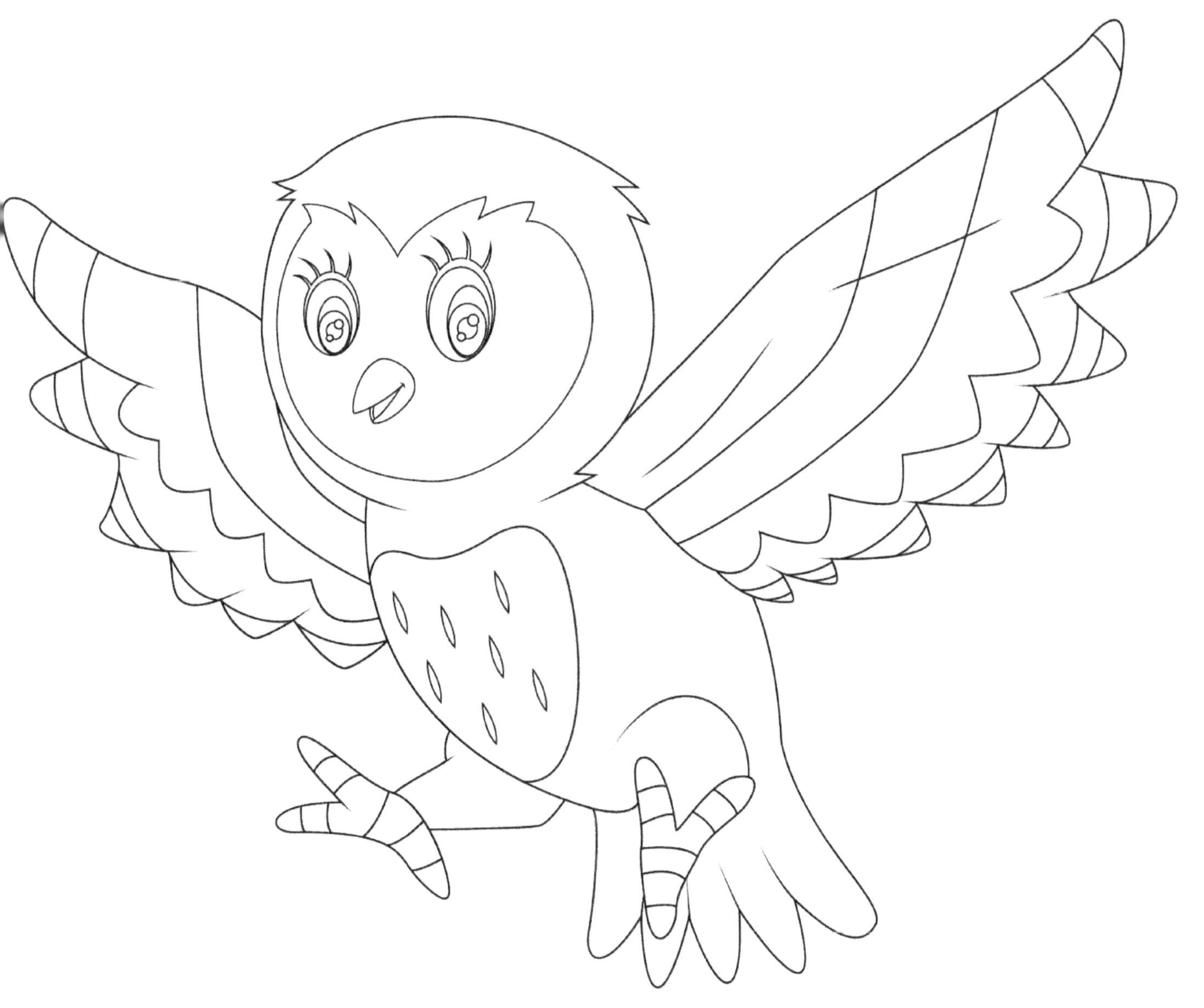

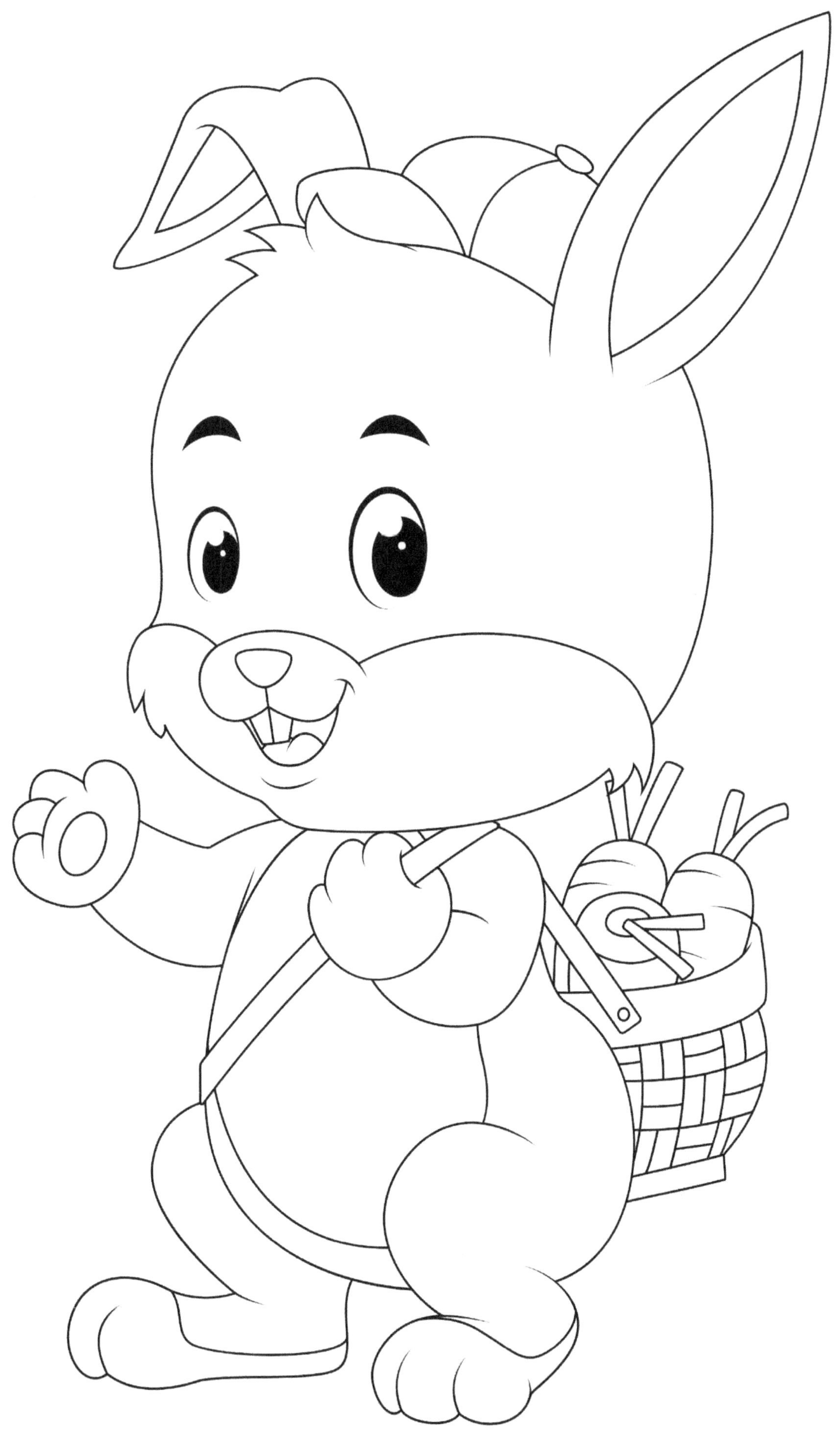

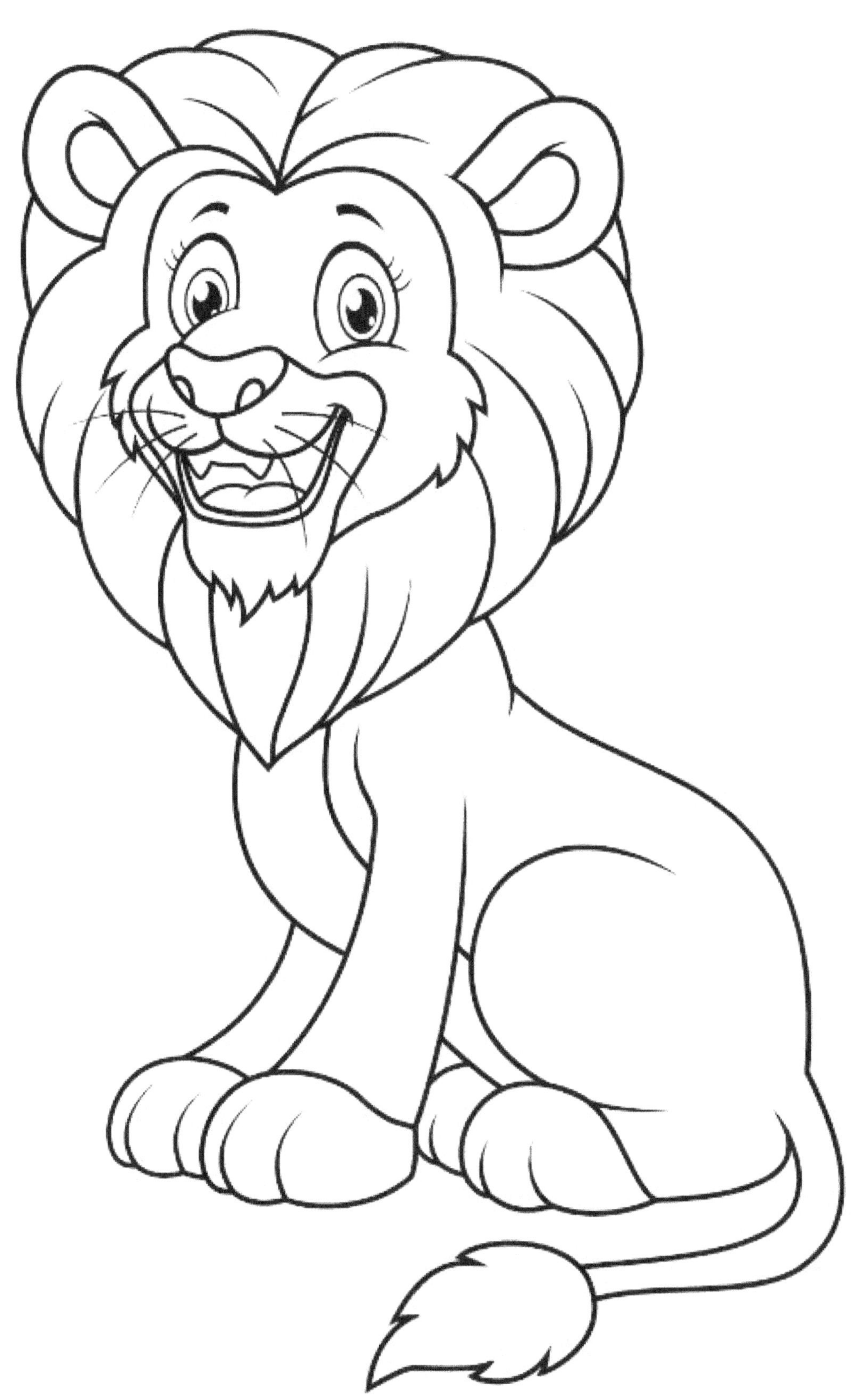

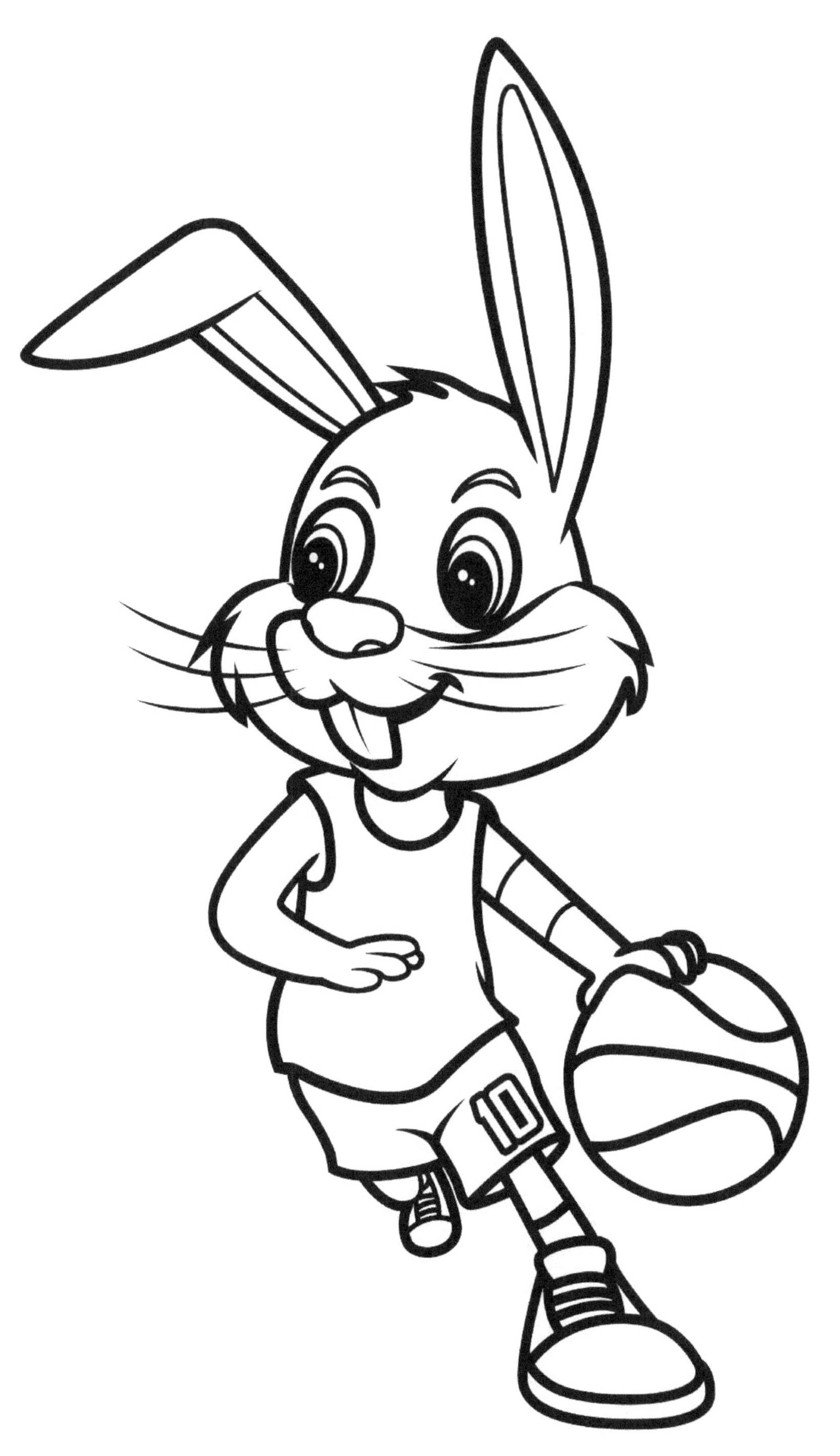

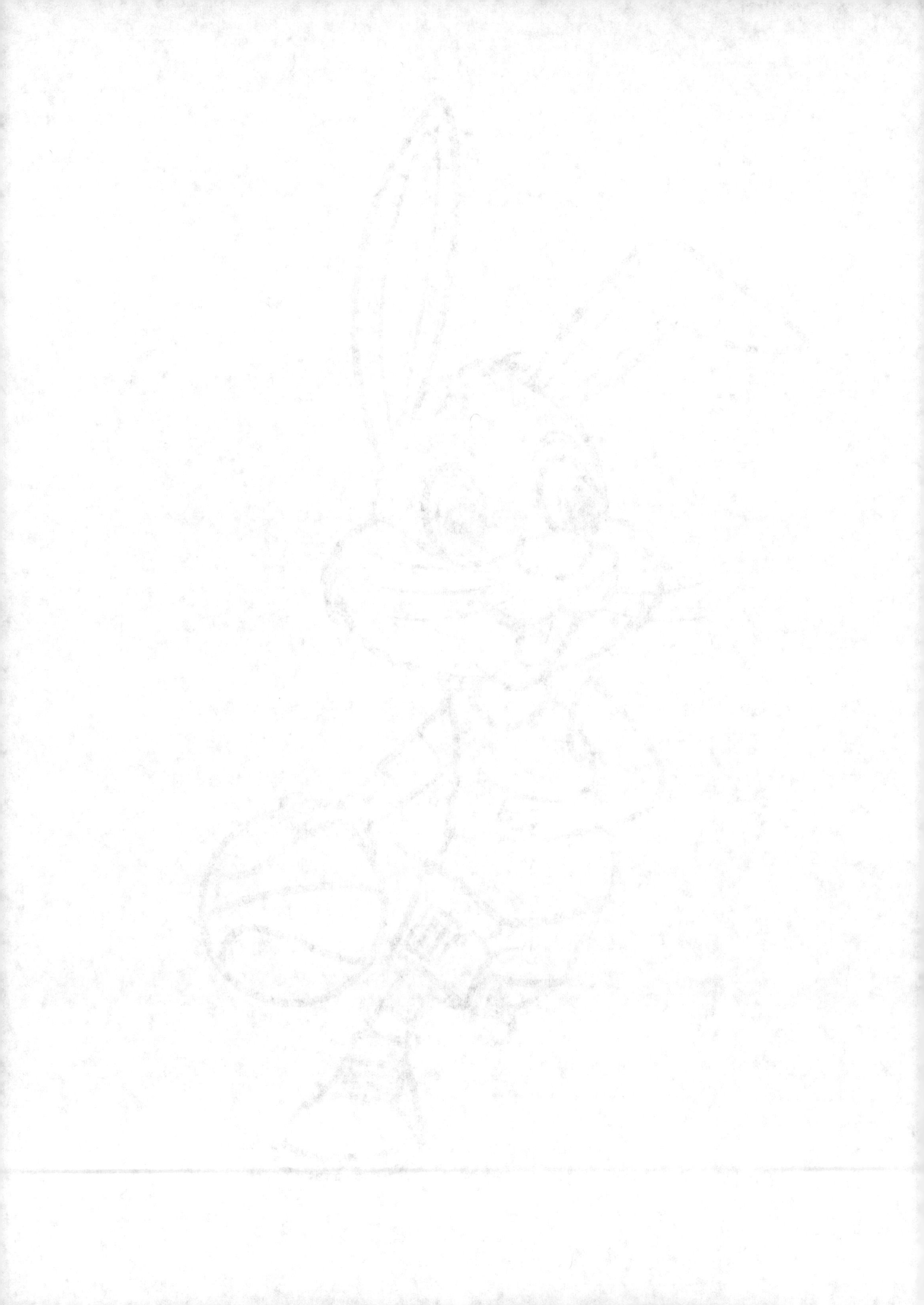

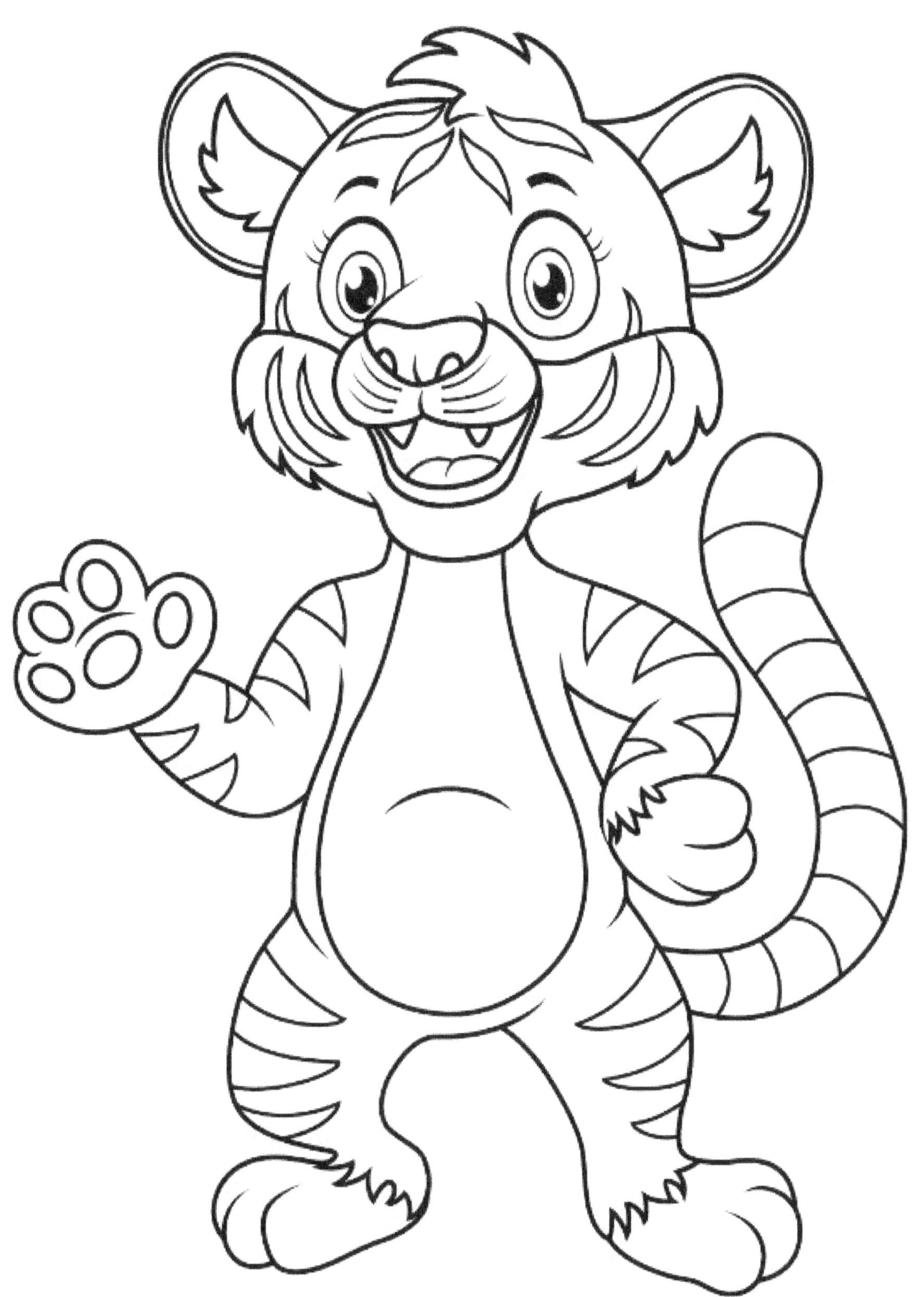

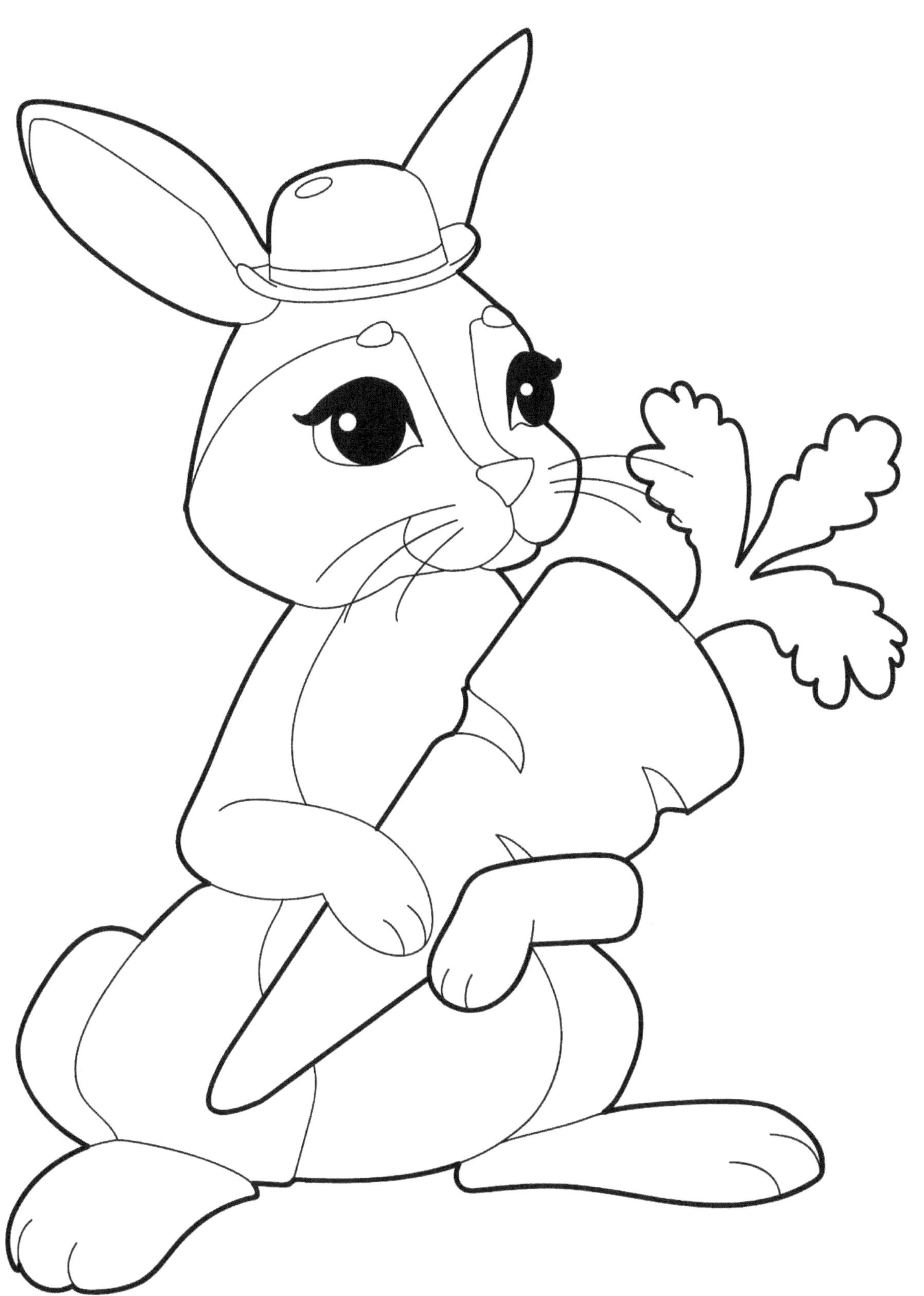

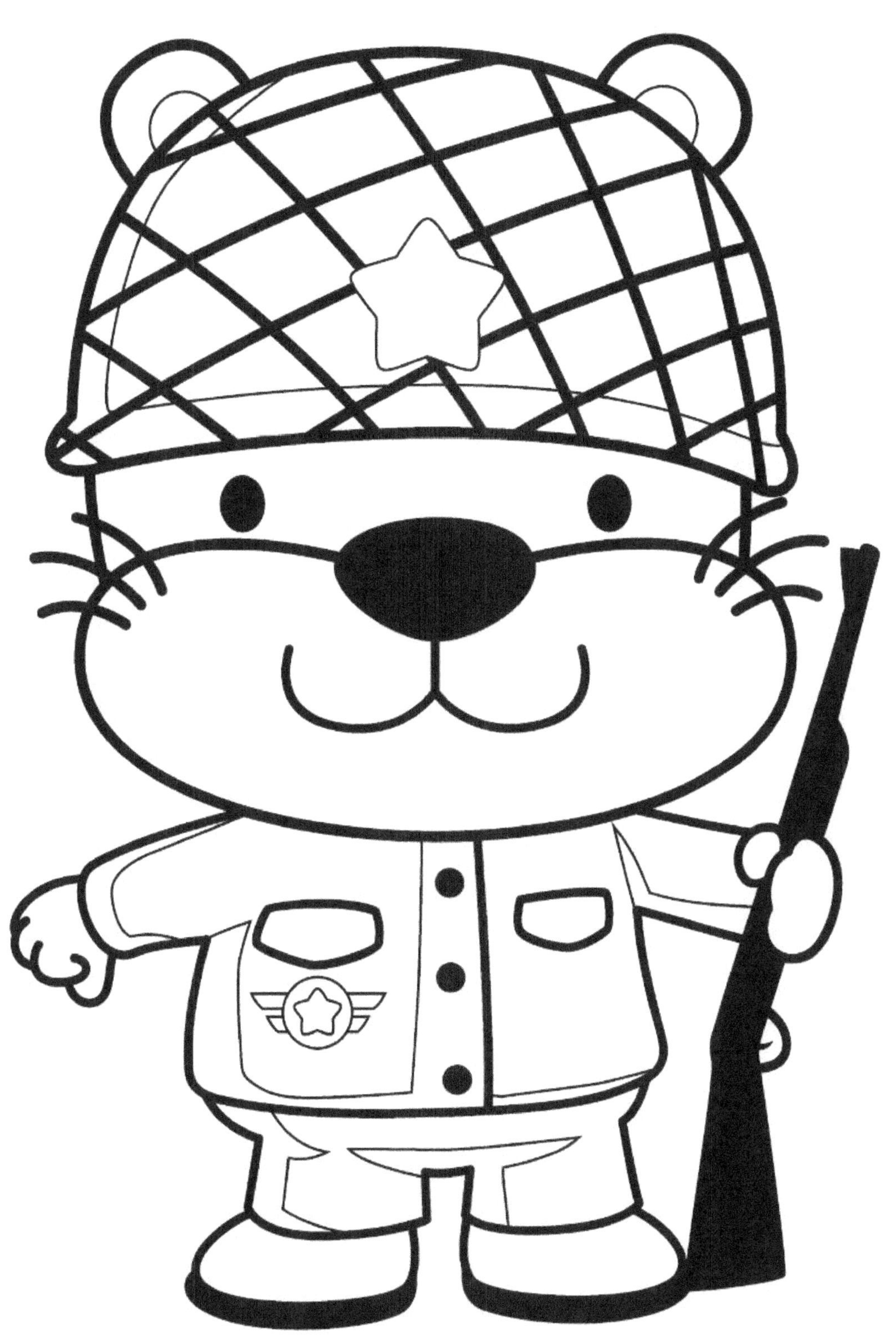

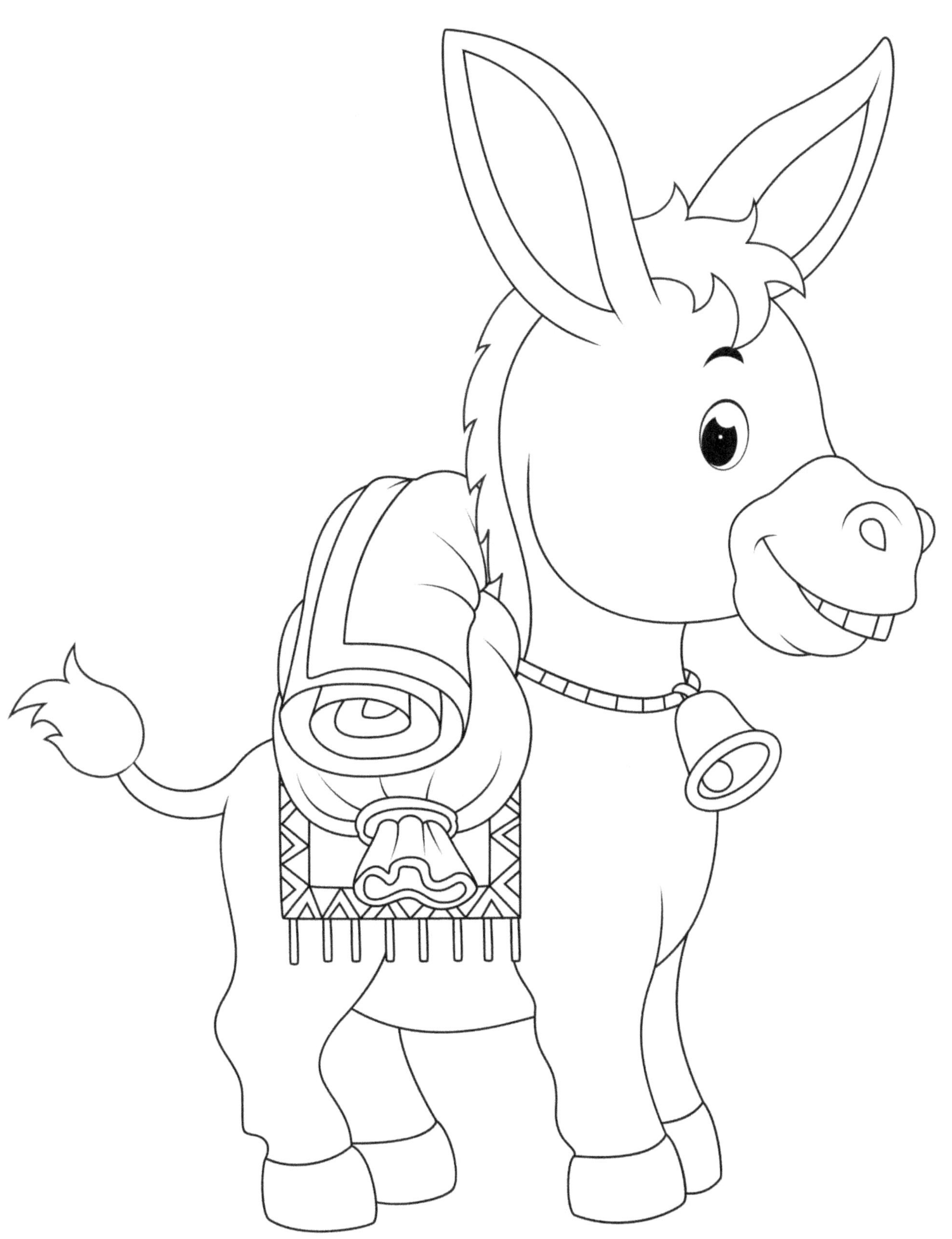

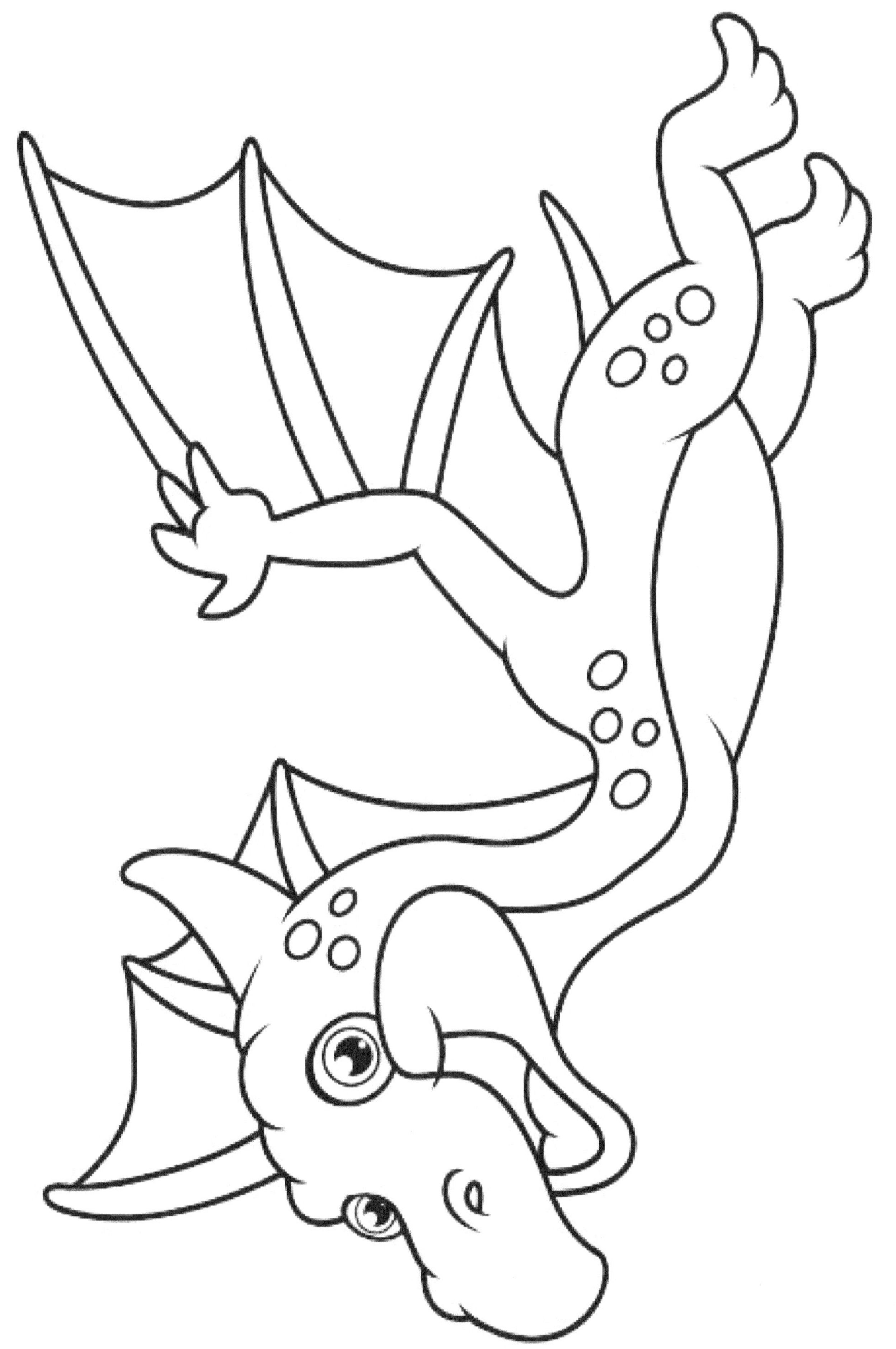

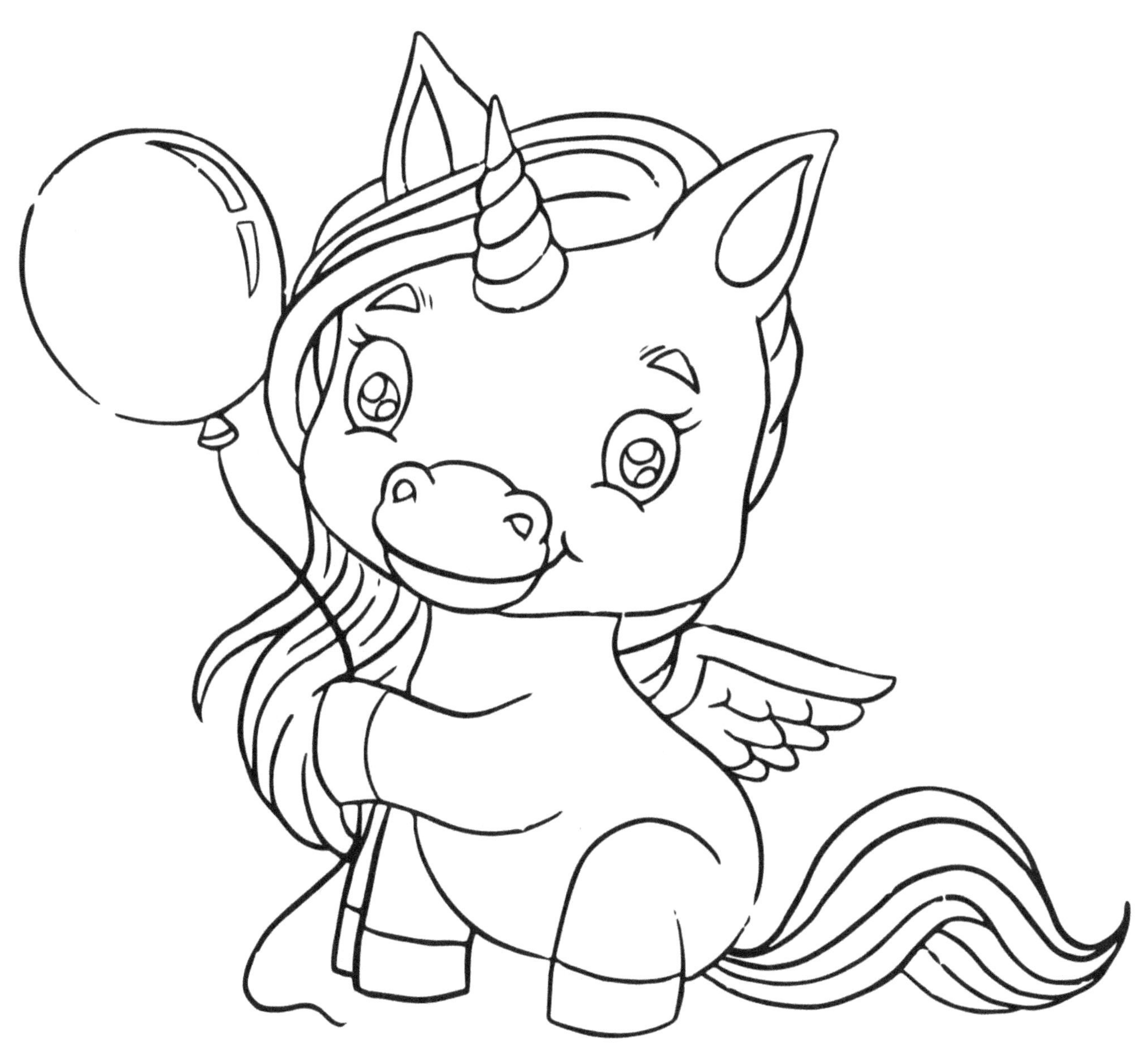

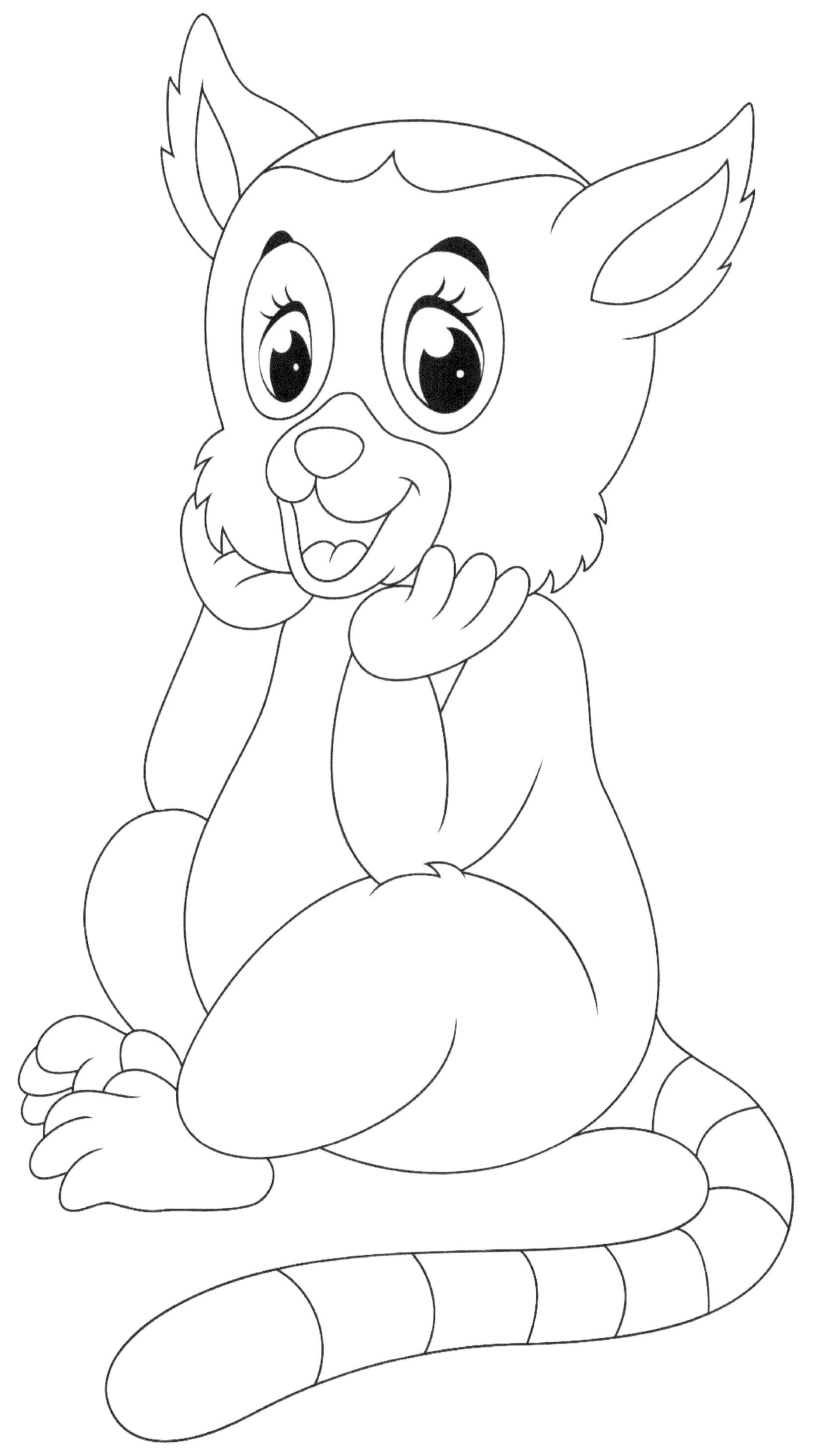